FINANCIAL INSTITUTIONS AND SERVICES

FAIR DEBT COLLECTION PRACTICES ACT

OVERVIEW, ANALYSES, AND ADMINISTRATION

FINANCIAL INSTITUTIONS AND SERVICES

Additional books in this series can be found on Nova's website under the Series tab.

Additional E-books in this series can be found on Nova's website under the E-book tab.

ECONOMIC ISSUES, PROBLEMS AND PERSPECTIVES

Additional books in this series can be found on Nova's website under the Series tab.

Additional E-books in this series can be found on Nova's website under the E-book tab.

FINANCIAL INSTITUTIONS AND SERVICES

FAIR DEBT COLLECTION PRACTICES ACT

OVERVIEW, ANALYSES, AND ADMINISTRATION

SVEN DE BOER
EDITOR

New York

For permission to use material from this book please contact us:
Telephone 631-231-7269; Fax 631-231-8175
Web Site: http://www.novapublishers.com

LIBRARY OF CONGRESS CATALOGING-IN-PUBLICATION DATA

ISBN: 978-1-62808-116-9

Published by Nova Science Publishers, Inc. † New York

CONTENTS

PREFACE

The recent fiscal crisis and recession have accentuated debt collection issues, prompted federal regulatory and enforcement activities regarding the debt collection industry, and motivated assessments of the effectiveness of the Fair Debt Collection Practices Act (FDCPA). The Consumer Financial Protection Bureau (CFPB) and the Federal Trade Commission (FTC), the two main agencies charged with regulating and/or enforcing the FDCPA, have identified debt buying, the use of litigation as a collection strategy, and the impact of current technology on the debt collection industry as three major developments that did not exist when the FDCPA was enacted in 1977. They have conducted analyses of consumer complaints about FDCPA violations and studies and workshops to evaluate the debt-buying industry and the impact of technological developments such as social media, email, mobile phones, etc., on how debt collectors communicate with consumers and find information about consumer debts. At present, about 30 million Americans, nearly 10% of the population, are subject to debt collection for amounts averaging $1,500 per person, according to the CFPB. This book provides an overview and analysis of the Fair Debt Collection Practices and Act with a focus on current issues and legislative proposals.

Chapter 1 – The recent fiscal crisis and recession have accentuated debt collection issues, prompted federal regulatory and enforcement activities regarding the debt collection industry, and motivated assessments of the effectiveness of the Fair Debt Collection Practices Act (FDCPA). The Consumer Financial Protection Bureau (Bureau or CFPB) and the Federal Trade Commission (FTC), the two main agencies charged with regulating and/or enforcing the FDCPA, have identified debt buying, the use of litigation as a collection strategy, and the impact of current technology on the debt collection industry as three major developments that did not exist when the FDCPA was enacted in 1977. They have conducted analyses of consumer complaints about FDCPA violations and studies and workshops to evaluate the debt-buying industry and the impact of technological developments such as social media, email, mobile phones, etc., on how debt collectors communicate with consumers and find information about consumer debts. At present, about 30 million Americans, nearly 10% of the population, are subject to debt collection for amounts averaging $1,500 per person, according to the CFPB.

The FDCPA was enacted as an amendment to the Consumer Credit Protection Act. Its purpose is to "eliminate abusive debt collection practices by debt collectors." Debt collectors are prohibited from threatening or harassing debtors, and their contacts with debtors are restricted. The FDCPA commonly only applies to third-party debt collectors. A "debt collector" is generally defined as "any person who uses any instrumentality of interstate commerce or the mails in any business the principal purpose of which is the collection of any debts, or who regularly collects or attempts to collect, directly or indirectly, debts owed or due or asserted to be owed or due another." The FDCPA does not apply to creditors who are collecting their own debts, unless in the process of collecting debts, the creditor uses a name other than his own which would indicate that a third person is attempting to collect the debt on his behalf. There are certain other exceptions, such as federal or state government employees collecting debts as part of their official duties.

As of the date of this report, only one bill to revise the FDCPA has been introduced in the 113th Congress. This bill would define child support as a debt. Several bills were introduced in the 112th Congress to address various consumer problems with the debt collection industry, including attempted collection of time-barred debts, arrests of debtors, inadequate information about a debt and/or inadequate verification of a debt, and threatening to withhold treatment to induce payment of delinquent medical debt. On the other hand, legislation in the 112th would also have restricted the liability of good-faith debt collectors for conduct that complies or conforms with regulations or interpretations of the CFPB.

Chapter 2 – The Consumer Financial Protection Bureau ("CFPB" or "the Bureau") is pleased to submit to Congress its second annual report summarizing its activities to administer the Fair Debt Collection Practices Act ("FDCPA" or "the Act"), 15 U.S.C. §§ 1692 *et seq.*, during the past year. These activities represent the Bureau's efforts to curtail deceptive, unfair, and abusive debt collection practices in the marketplace.

Last year the Bureau issued its inaugural annual report to Congress, following the Dodd-Frank Act's transfer of responsibility from the Federal Trade Commission ("FTC") to the Bureau. The FTC had previously prepared this report annually since the FDCPA's enactment in 1977. Under the Dodd-Frank Act, the Bureau has primary government responsibility for administering the FDCPA. The Bureau has the authority to prescribe rules with respect to debt collection; issue guidance concerning compliance with the law; collect complaint data; educate consumers and collectors; and undertake research and policy initiatives related to consumer debt collection. The Bureau shares overall enforcement responsibility with the FTC and other federal agencies.

Over the past year, the Bureau and the FTC have continued to collaborate in the area of debt collection. Consistent with those efforts, the FTC has provided the Bureau with a letter summarizing its debt collection activities during the past year. As in previous years, the FTC took significant steps in 2012 to curtail illegal debt collection practices. Information about the FTC's activities is incorporated into this report, and the FTC's letter is included in this report as Appendix A. The Bureau is grateful to the FTC for its assistance with this annual report.

This report (1) provides background on the FDCPA and the debt collection market; (2) summarizes the Bureau's Consumer Response function and the number and types of consumer complaints regarding debt collection received by the FTC in 2012; (3) describes the Bureau's supervision program as it relates to debt collection; (4) presents recent developments in the Bureau and FTC's law enforcement and advocacy programs; (5) discusses recent education and outreach initiatives; (6) discusses recent research and policy initiatives; and (7) discusses coordination and cooperation between the Bureau and the FTC in the administration of the FDCPA.

In: Fair Debt Collection Practices Act
Editor: Sven De Boer
ISBN: 978-1-62808-116-9

Chapter 1

Fair Debt Collection Practices Act (FDCPA)*

Margaret Mikyung Lee

Summary

The recent fiscal crisis and recession have accentuated debt collection issues, prompted federal regulatory and enforcement activities regarding the debt collection industry, and motivated assessments of the effectiveness of the Fair Debt Collection Practices Act (FDCPA). The Consumer Financial Protection Bureau (Bureau or CFPB) and the Federal Trade Commission (FTC), the two main agencies charged with regulating and/or enforcing the FDCPA, have identified debt buying, the use of litigation as a collection strategy, and the impact of current technology on the debt collection industry as three major developments that did not exist when the FDCPA was enacted in 1977. They have conducted analyses of consumer complaints about FDCPA violations and studies and workshops to evaluate the debt-buying industry and the impact of technological developments such as social media, email, mobile phones, etc., on how debt collectors communicate with consumers and find information about consumer debts. At present, about 30 million Americans, nearly 10% of the population, are subject to debt collection for amounts averaging $1,500 per person, according to the CFPB.

---

* This is an edited, reformatted and augmented version of the Congressional Research Service Publication, CRS Report for Congress R43041, dated April 11, 2013.

The FDCPA was enacted as an amendment to the Consumer Credit Protection Act. Its purpose is to "eliminate abusive debt collection practices by debt collectors." Debt collectors are prohibited from threatening or harassing debtors, and their contacts with debtors are restricted. The FDCPA commonly only applies to third-party debt collectors. A "debt collector" is generally defined as "any person who uses any instrumentality of interstate commerce or the mails in any business the principal purpose of which is the collection of any debts, or who regularly collects or attempts to collect, directly or indirectly, debts owed or due or asserted to be owed or due another." The FDCPA does not apply to creditors who are collecting their own debts, unless in the process of collecting debts, the creditor uses a name other than his own which would indicate that a third person is attempting to collect the debt on his behalf. There are certain other exceptions, such as federal or state government employees collecting debts as part of their official duties.

As of the date of this report, only one bill to revise the FDCPA has been introduced in the 113th Congress. This bill would define child support as a debt. Several bills were introduced in the 112th Congress to address various consumer problems with the debt collection industry, including attempted collection of time-barred debts, arrests of debtors, inadequate information about a debt and/or inadequate verification of a debt, and threatening to withhold treatment to induce payment of delinquent medical debt. On the other hand, legislation in the 112th would also have restricted the liability of good-faith debt collectors for conduct that complies or conforms with regulations or interpretations of the CFPB.

INTRODUCTION

The recent fiscal crisis and recession have accentuated debt collection issues, prompted federal regulatory and enforcement activities regarding the debt collection industry, and motivated assessments of the effectiveness of the Fair Debt Collection Practices Act (FDCPA).[1] The Consumer Financial Protection Bureau (Bureau or CFPB) and the Federal Trade Commission (FTC), the two main agencies charged with regulating and/or enforcing the FDCPA, have identified debt buying, the use of litigation as a collection strategy, and the impact of current technology on the debt collection industry as three major developments that did not exist when the FDCPA was enacted in 1977.[2] They have conducted analyses of consumer complaints about FDCPA violations, studies on and workshops to evaluate the debt buying industry, and the impact of technological developments such as social media, email, and mobile phones on how debt collectors communicate with consumers and find information about consumer debts.[3] At present, about 30 million Americans, nearly 10% of the population, are subject to debt collection for amounts averaging $1,500 per person, according to the CFPB.[4]

The FDCPA was signed into law on September 29, 1977, as an amendment to the Consumer Credit Protection Act.[5] The purpose of the FDCPA is to "eliminate abusive debt collection practices by debt collectors."[6] Debt collectors are prohibited from threatening or harassing debtors, and their contacts with debtors are restricted. The FDCPA commonly only applies to third-party debt collectors. A "debt collector" is generally defined as "any person who uses any instrumentality of interstate commerce or the mails in any business the principal purpose of which is the collection of any debts, or who regularly collects or attempts to collect, directly or indirectly, debts owed or due or asserted to be owed or due another."[7] The FDCPA does not apply to creditors who are collecting their own debts, unless in the process of collecting debts, the creditor uses a name other than his own which would indicate that a third person is attempting to collect the debt on his behalf.[8] The FDCPA defines certain other exceptions to "debt collector," such as a person collecting debt for a creditor related by common ownership or corporate control as long as the person only collects debts for such related creditors and is not principally engaged in the debt collection business;[9] federal or state government employees collecting debts as part of their official duties;[10] a person serving legal process in judicial enforcement of a debt;[11] a bona- fide, non-profit credit counseling organization that assists consumers by receiving and disbursing their debt payments to creditors;[12] and private entities that administer certain pretrial diversion programs for bad check offenders under a contract with a state or district attorney.[13]

The CFPB is a relatively new agency. Establishing the CFPB pursuant to the Consumer Financial Protection Act of 2010,[14] which is part of the Dodd-Frank Wall Street Reform and Consumer Protection Act (Dodd-Frank Act),[15] Congress transferred administrative functions, including rulemaking and reporting on debt collection activities, as well as certain enforcement functions, from other federal agencies such as the FTC and the Federal Reserve Board, to the Bureau.[16] The FTC and other agencies, however, retain and share enforcement authority with the CFPB[17] and the CFPB and FTC coordinate their enforcement activities.[18]

Overview of the FDCPA

Prohibited Actions

Under the FDCPA, absent the consumer's prior consent, a debt collector is prohibited from contacting the consumer at any unusual or inconvenient time or place.[19] Contacts are limited to between the times of 8:00 am and 9:00 pm, and a debt collector may not contact the consumer at his place of employment "if the debt collector knows or has reason to know that the consumer's employer prohibits the consumer from receiving such communication."[20] If the consumer is represented by an attorney in connection with the debt owed, the debt collector may only contact the attorney, unless the attorney consents to direct communication with the consumer.[21]

While collecting or attempting to collect a debt, a debt collector may not harass or abuse a consumer. Specifically, the FDCPA prohibits use or threats of violence to harm the physical person, reputation, or property of the consumer.[22] Debt collectors are prohibited from using obscene or profane language and cannot repeatedly call the consumer with the intent to annoy, abuse, or harass.[23] Debt collectors must also identify themselves when contacting the consumer by telephone.[24] If a consumer notifies a debt collector that the consumer refuses to pay the debt or that he wishes the debt collector to cease communication, the debt collector is prohibited from contacting the consumer, except to notify the consumer that the communication will stop or that the debt collector or creditor intends to take further action.[25]

Debt collectors are prohibited from communicating with third parties regarding the consumer's debt except for the purpose of locating the consumer.[26] When making such contacts, the debt collector must identify himself and state that he is confirming or correcting location information concerning the consumer, and is prohibited from disclosing to the third party that the consumer owes any debt.[27] In general, debt collectors may contact third parties only once.[28] The FDCPA also prohibits publication of lists of consumers who allegedly refuse to pay debts, except to a consumer reporting agency, as well as the advertisement for sale of any debt to coerce payment of the debt.[29]

Debt collectors are also prohibited from using any false, deceptive, or misleading representation or means in connection with the collection of any debt.[30] This prohibition includes, but is not limited to, false representation that the debt collector is affiliated with the United States or any state government, or the false representation about the legal status of the debt or the legal consequences of not paying the debt.[31] In addition, a debt collector may not use unfair or unconscionable means to collect or attempt to collect any debt, including the collection of unauthorized charges, the deposit of postdated checks, and taking or threatening to take nonjudicial action to take property from the consumer.[32]

Requirements for Debt Collectors

Within five days of the initial communication with a consumer, a debt collector is required to send the consumer a written notice containing the following information: the amount of the debt; the name of the creditor to whom the debt is owed; a statement informing the consumer of the right to dispute the validity of the debt within 30 days; a statement that if the consumer notifies the debt collector of the dispute within 30 days, the debt collector will obtain verification of the debt and mail the verification to the consumer; and a statement that, upon the consumer's request, the debt collector will provide the consumer with the name and address of the original creditor if different from the current creditor.[33] Neither a formal pleading in a civil action nor a form/notice unrelated to debt collection and expressly required by the Internal Revenue Code, Title V of the Gramm-Leach-Bliley Act, or any federal/state law related to data breach or privacy, shall be treated as an initial communication for debt collection.[34]

If the consumer notifies the debt collector within the 30-day time period that he or she disputes the debt or requests the name and address of the original creditor, the debt collector is required to cease collection of the debt, or the disputed portion thereof, until the debt collector obtains verification of the debt.[35] If a consumer owes multiple debts, a debt collector is required to apply any payments the consumer makes as the consumer directs, and may not apply such payments to any debt the consumer disputes.[36]

Remedies Available

Debt collectors who violate any provision of the FDCPA are subject to civil liability. A consumer may bring a private cause of action under the FDCPA within one year of the date of the violation in any appropriate United States district court or any other court of competent jurisdiction. A consumer may recover his or her actual damages as well as additional damages not to exceed $1,000 in addition to court costs and attorney's fees.[37] In determining the amount of liability, courts consider the frequency and persistence of the debt collector's noncompliance, the nature of the noncompliance, and the extent to which the noncompliance was intentional.[38] In addition to private remedies, the FTC and other federal agencies enforce the FDCPA through injunctive relief and civil penalties.[39]

AGENCY ACTIVITIES

Regulation, Supervision, and Policy

Pursuant to the Dodd-Frank Act, the CFPB has regulatory, supervisory, and enforcement authority for the FDCPA[40] although it also shares supervisory and enforcement authority with other agencies that oversee financial services businesses.[41] Under the Dodd-Frank Act, the CFPB oversees consumer financial protection laws with respect to certain nonbank covered persons that offer specified consumer financial products, including residential mortgages, private educational loans, and payday loans, and also their service providers, such as third-party debt collectors.[42] The Dodd-Frank Act also authorizes the CFPB to supervise "larger participants" with respect to other consumer financial products or services.[43]

Accordingly, in October 2012, the CFPB promulgated a final rule, effective January 2, 2013, defining larger participants in the consumer debt collection market as those whose annual receipts from consumer debt collection exceed $10 million.[44] The Bureau observed that larger participants in the consumer debt collection market generally include entities such as third-party debt collectors, debt buyers, and collection attorneys.[45] It estimates that approximately 175 firms, 4% of the market, comprise the larger, nonbank participants in the consumer debt collection market and account for 63% of the annual receipts from the market.[46]

The Bureau noted that the rule did not delineate the scope of federal laws on debt collection; that some activities not covered by the rule may constitute "debt collection" under the Dodd-Frank Act and be subject to the FDCPA; and that nonbank covered persons generally are subject to the Bureau's regulatory and enforcement authority under the FDCPA and other federal consumer financial laws regardless of whether they are subject to the Bureau's supervisory authority.[47] The CFPB further noted that it has authority to supervise first-party debt collection activities of many covered persons, such as banks, credit unions, and their affiliates, despite the fact that such activities are not covered by this rule.[48]

The CFPB followed the FDCPA in defining "debt collector" in the rule. Under the rule, a debt collector is a person whose principal business activity is debt collection or who regularly engages in debt collection.[49] Accordingly, although the rule does not exclude attorneys categorically from the "debt collector" definition, an attorney who occasionally files a claim or counter-claim against a consumer would not appear to constitute a debt collector under the rule.[50]

Also in October 2012, the CFPB issued *CFPB Debt Collection Examinations Procedures* to provide guidance on auditing bank and nonbank debt collection activities. In these guidelines, the CFPB stated that its examiners will "evaluate the quality of the regulated entity's compliance management systems, review practices to ensure they comply with federal consumer financial law, and identify risks to consumers throughout the debt collection process."[51]

The CFPB and FTC have been studying debt collection markets in order to develop policy initiatives. By reducing lender/creditor losses, debt markets arguably enable lender/creditors to extend more credit at lower interest rates. In January 2013, the FTC published the first major empirical study of the market for debt based on information from the nine largest debt-buying companies in the United States.[52] Covering about 76% of the industry, the study evaluated more than 5,000 portfolios comprising about 90 million consumer accounts with a face value of $143 billion (purchased for about $6.5 billion).[53] About 71% of the debt was credit-card debt. Credit- card debt also constituted 62% of all portfolios and 71% of the total amount that the debt buyers spent to purchase debt.[54] In the study, purchasers of debt paid an average of about 4 cents on the dollar and older debt sold for less than newer debt.[55] The study found that consumers annually disputed an estimated 1 million or more debts, or 3.2% of the total that debt buyers sought to collect.[56] Interestingly, debt buyers verified only about half, or about 500,000, of these disputed debts.[57]

Disputes over debt and the failure of debt buyers to verify disputed debt could be linked to the study's finding that debt buyers had limited information on the debt at the time they purchased it. The study found that, at the time of a debt purchase, creditors provided debt buyers with some information about the debts, including the debtor's personal information (name, address, telephone number, and social security number of the debtor) and the debtor's account information (the account number, date it was opened, date of the debtor's last payment, and the outstanding balance).[58] However, certain key information was not provided, such as prior consumer disputes over the debt or prior verifications of debts by collectors.[59] Moreover, most debt buying contracts provided that creditors did not warrant that information they gave to buyers was accurate.[60] While debt buyers generally knew the age of the debt purchased,[61] some of the debt sold was barred from collection by state statutes of limitations, which typically provided between three and six years to collect credit card debt.[62]

The report did not answer questions,[63] including (1) why debt buyers did not disclose more information to consumers with validation notices; (2) why they did not seek additional information post-purchase; and (3) why they did not verify nearly half of the disputed debts. The report also did not evaluate debt buyer practices in bringing legal actions to collect debts or examine the accuracy of information debt buyers receive and use to collect debts. The study also did not include data from any smaller debt buyers. The report noted, however, that this information would be useful for further studies of the debt buying market.[64]

In addition to the FTC report, both the CFPB and the FTC sought information through individual meetings and participation at conferences from other industry stakeholders, including other debt collectors, lenders/creditors, consumer advocacy groups, state regulators, and technology experts. For example, in the CFPB 2013 Report, the FTC particularly noted a workshop it convened in 2011 to discuss the role and impact of technology in the debt collection market, *Debt Collection 2.0: Protecting Consumers as Technologies Change*.[65] The workshop covered issues such as use of collection software and databases in handling and maintaining information on debtors and their accounts and use of mobile phones, voicemail, answering machines, texting, email, and social media in communicating with debtors and in finding information, including location, about debtors.[66] The participants also discussed how litigation may impact use of such technologies and possible avenues for legislation and regulation to address appropriate use of debt collection technology that did not exist when the FDCPA was originally enacted in 1977.[67]

Enforcement

The CFPB and FTC coordinate FDCPA enforcement activities.[68] Under the FDCPA, the FTC treats FDCPA violations as violations of the Federal

Trade Commission Act (FTCA) rules and uses its FTCA powers to enforce FDCPA compliance.[69] The Dodd-Frank Act authorizes the Bureau to prohibit unfair, deceptive, or abusive acts or practices in connection with any consumer financial product or service, or any offer of a consumer financial product or service.[70] The FTCA similarly authorizes the FTC to prohibit unfair methods of competition and unfair or deceptive acts or practices in or affecting commerce.[71]

The CFPB and the FTC reported on enforcement issues and plans during 2012.[72] The FTC reported that it received a range of consumer complaints about debt collection and categorized them by types comprising subcategories of violations that correlate to FDCPA prohibited acts.[73] The FTC noted several points about these statistics: (1) they only include complaints received directly by the FTC; (2) the number of complaints may understate the extent of FDCPA violations since many consumers may complain to other agencies or the creditor, or they are not aware that certain practices are illegal; and (3) not all complaints involve illegal practices.[74] It is worth noting that the FTC does not intervene in individual consumer complaints.[75] Rather, it uses complaints that it receives to monitor, evaluate, and target debt-collector conduct for investigation and possible civil penalties.[76]

In contrast, the CFPB's mission includes responding to individual consumer complaints.[77] Although the CFPB is gradually expanding the scope of consumer complaints that it handles, including addressing credit report complaints, it has not yet begun to accept and address debt collection complaints from individual consumers pursuant to its FDCPA authority.[78] However, it has already begun to bring enforcement actions for violations that have come to its attention by other means.

In October 2012, the CFPB brought its first public enforcement action for debt collection practices against three American Express affiliates.[79] Because these affiliates were first-party debt collectors, the Bureau brought the action pursuant to its Dodd-Frank Act authority to prohibit unfair, deceptive, or abusive acts or practices rather than under its FDCPA authority.[80] In this action, the CFPB found that American Express deceived consumers by telling them that debt payment would be reported to consumer reporting agencies, thereby improving the consumers' credit scores, notwithstanding that the debts were so old that they could no longer appear on credit reports and thus would not affect credit scores.[81] The company also deceptively told consumers that if they accepted settlement offers their debt would be forgiven and they would be issued new American Express cards.[82] Pursuant to the enforcement action, American Express paid full restitution plus interest to consumers who were told that paying the debt would improve their credit scores. In addition to refunding any payments made on debt that had been forgiven, American Express also paid $100 and provided a pre-approved card to each consumer that had been denied a new card despite having settled with American Express.[83] Prospectively, American Express must disclose to consumers when older debt is time-barred from collection litigation or credit reports.[84] American Express was also barred from collecting debt when it does not have adequate documentation of the debt[85] and assessed civil penalties totaling $14.1 million for deceptive debt collection and other legal violations.[86]

The FTC has also brought enforcement actions against debt collectors that engage in unfair or deceptive acts or practices in violation of the FTCA or the FDCPA. In recent years, the FTC has increased such activities and sought stronger penalties and remedies in order to improve deterrence.[87] In 2012, the FTC brought or resolved seven debt collection cases, equaling the highest number of cases it has brought or resolved in any given year.[88] These cases involved false threats, harassment, or abuse; attempts to collect phantom debts (alleged debts that do not exist or which the debt collector has no right to collect), which also involved overseas call centers, collectors falsely claiming to be law enforcement personnel and threatening arrest; and time- barred debt.[89] In resolving these actions, the FTC imposed remedies, ranging from monetary redress for consumers, civil penalties, restraining orders with asset freezes, preliminary and permanent injunctions against violations of the FTCA and FDCPA.[90] One case involved parallel criminal proceedings for wire and mail fraud related to phantom debt collection.[91]

Aside from typical enforcement activities, The CFPB and FTC also advocate on behalf of consumers by filing amicus briefs in cases involving debt collection practices. Recently, in *Marx v. General Revenue Corporation*,[92] the U.S. Supreme Court held that a consumer plaintiff who loses a lawsuit brought under the FDCPA could be ordered to pay the defendant debt collector's court costs, other than attorney's fees, even when the consumer brought the lawsuit in good faith and it was not frivolous. The CFPB, FTC, and U.S. Department of Justice (DOJ) had jointly filed an amicus brief with the Court urging it to rule that consumer plaintiffs who lose a good-faith lawsuit for FDCPA violations are not required to pay costs for the defendant debt collector.[93] In part, the federal government argued that imposing litigation costs on losing consumer plaintiffs who bring a good-faith lawsuit, rather than limiting it to those who bring bad-faith, harassing suits, would discourage consumers from bringing private lawsuits.[94] This, in turn, would undermine congressional intent to deter unlawful debt collection practices via private enforcement actions.[95]

ISSUES AND LEGISLATIVE PROPOSALS

In addition to the problems noted in the CFPB report and the exclusion of first-party debt collectors from FDCPA coverage,[96] several issues have arisen regarding the FDCPA, its implementation and enforcement, and activities beyond the scope of federal consumer protection. Consumer advocates have identified problems such as inadequate verification of debt[97] and arbitration clauses that limit consumer ability to litigate potentially illegal debt collection practices.[98] In addition, consumer advocates have criticized arrests of debtors for failure to comply with default judgments affirming debts and ordering payment, as being tantamount to a revival of "debtor's prison."[99] Other commentators have criticized FDCPA debt collector treatment such as judicial FDCPA interpretations limiting bona-fide errors as defense to FDCPA violations[100] and limits on voicemail/autodialing to contact consumers regarding debt collection.[101]

In recent years, some of the issues discussed above have been addressed in proposed legislation although none advanced beyond introduction. As of the date of this report, one bill to revise the FDCPA has been introduced in the 113th Congress. S. 508 would define child support as a debt and is similar to S. 1383 in the 112th Congress.[102] Among the various bills introduced in the 112th Congress to address consumer debt collection, H.R. 2361 would have prohibited a debt collector from bringing or threatening to bring a lawsuit against a consumer to collect a time-barred debt and required a debt collector to disclose to a consumer that (1) a time-barred debt has been sold to the debt collector by the creditor; (2) the collector may not sue the consumer for payment of the debt because the statute of limitations has expired; and (3) any payment by the consumer on the debt may restart the clock on the statute of limitations.[103] S. 3350 would have, among other things, prohibited a debt collector from requesting a court or agency to issue a warrant for the arrest of a debtor; reduced inadequate information about a debt by requiring a debt collector to disclose certain debt information to a consumer; reduced inadequate verification of a debt by requiring a debt collector to conduct a thorough investigation of a disputed debt and give a timely response to the consumer with specific information and verification of the debt; and prohibited threatening to withhold medical treatment to induce payment of delinquent medical debt.[104] H.R. 1783/S. 824 would have amended the FDCPA to cover a securitized residential mortgage and its servicer, and expanded civil liability to cover a debt collector who violates the FDCPA with regard to a debt secured by a consumer's residence.[105]

FDCPA Complaint Category	Total 2012 Complaints	Percentage of 2012 FDCPA Complaints	2012 Category Rank	Total 2011 Complaints	Percentage of 2011 FDCPA Complaints	2011 Category Rank
Misrepresent Debt Character, Amount, or Status	39,993	38.9%	1	47,012	39.5%	2
Repeated Calls	37,543	36.5%	2	47,573	40.0%	1
Falsely Threatens Illegal or Unintended Act	30,470	29.6%	3	35,738	30.0%	3
No Written Notice	26,139	25.4%	4	30,753	25.9%	4
Falsely Threatens Arrest, Property Seizure	24,062	23.4%	5	27,270	22.9%	5
Fails to Identify as Debt Collector	17,873	17.4%	6	20,793	17.5%	6
Repeated Calls to Third Parties	16,679	16.2%	7	20,798	17.5%	7
Improperly Calls Debtor At Work	14,482	14.1%	8	16,932	14.2%	8
Uses Obscene, Profane, or Abusive Language	13,329	13.0%	9	16,610	14.0%	9
Reveals Debt to Third Party	12,272	11.9%	10	12,654	10.6%	10
Refuses to Verify Debt After Written Request	9,814	9.5%	11	10,002	8.4%	12
Collects Unauthorized Fees, Interest, or Expenses	9,034	8.8%	12	9,325	7.8%	13
Calls Before 8:00 a.m., after 9:00 p.m., or at Inconvenient Times	8,166	7.9%	13	10,494	8.8%	11
Calls Debtor After Getting "Cease Communication" Notice	4,928	4.8%	14	5,933	5.0%	14
Uses or Threatens Violence	3,312	3.2%	15	3,980	3.3%	15

Source: The FTC, as submitted to and reported by the CFPB in its 2013 Report, *supra* note 2.

Notes: The CFPB does not yet accept debt collection complaints, although it is gradually expanding the scope of its complaint handling and plans to include debt collection. The FTC receives FDCPA-related complaints and reported these statistics to the CFPB.

Figure 1. FDCPA Complaint Type, Number, and Percentage in 2012 and 2011.

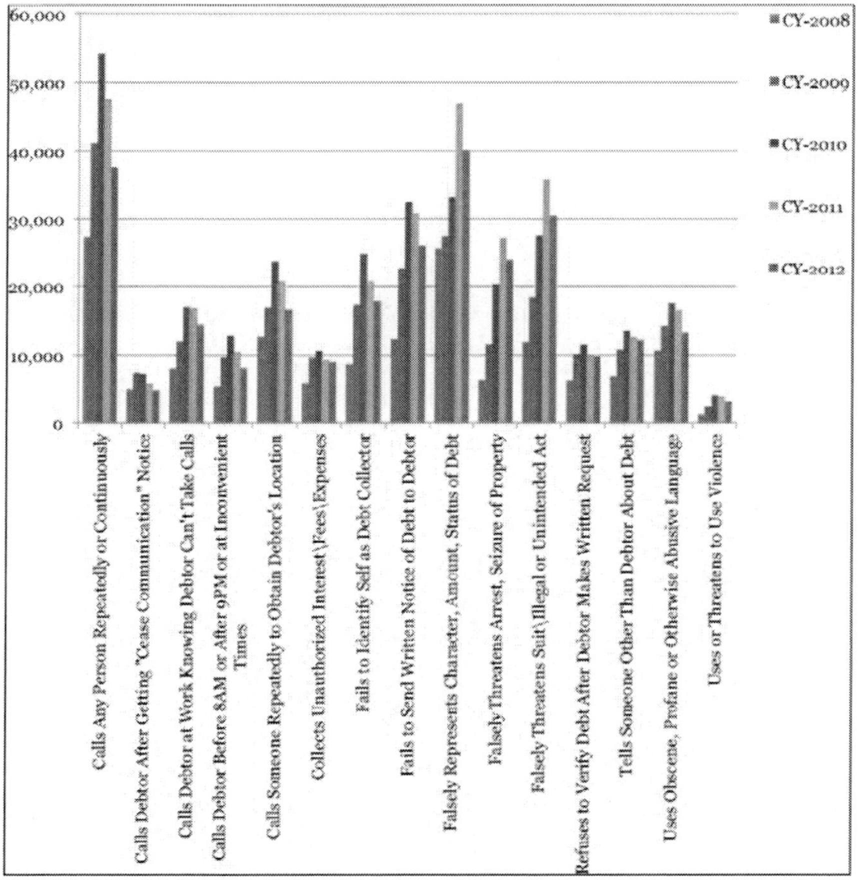

Source: CFPB, FDCPA Annual Report 2013, *supra* note 2.

Figure 2. Number of Complaints Received in Each Debt Collection Practice Category, 2008–2012.

To address debt collector problems, H.R. 4101/H.R. 5794 would have limited debt collector liability for conduct that the debt collector in good faith believed complied or conformed to regulations or official interpretations of the CFPB that were later amended, rescinded, or determined to be invalid by a judicial or other authority.[106] It also would have permitted a debt collector to leave messages for a consumer relating to debt collection on a telephone answering machine, voicemail system, or similar device, including an initial communication, as long as the message complies with regulations to ensure consumer privacy, including restrictions on third- party communications.

Finally, H.R. 4101/H.R. 5794 would have prohibited use of arbitration to resolve a debt collection dispute unless the consumer has agreed to arbitration in writing after debt collection activities have begun and a lawsuit or dispute has arisen.

End Notes

[1] P.L. 95-109, 91 Stat. 874, codified as amended at 15 U.S.C. §§1692 *et. seq.*
[2] CFPB Annual Report 2013, *Fair Debt Collection Practices Act*, at 9 (March 20, 2013) [*hereinafter* 2013 Report].
[3] *See* discussion *infra* notes 52, 65, and 72 and accompanying text.
[4] *Id.* at 2.
[5] *Id.*
[6] 15 U.S.C. §1692(e).
[7] *Id.* §1692a(6).
[8] *Id.*
[9] *Id.* §1692a(6)(B).
[10] *Id.* §1692a(6)(C).
[11] *Id.* §1692a(6)(D).
[12] *Id.* §1692a(6)(E).
[13] *Id.* §1692p.
[14] P.L. 111-203, Title X, §§1001–1100H, 124 Stat. 1376–2113 (2010).
[15] P.L. 111-203, 124 Stat. 1376 (2010).
[16] *Id.* §§1024-1027, 1029, and 1061 establish CFPB functions and transfer functions to the CFPB from other federal financial services agencies and the FTC. The changes to administrative enforcement authority for the FDCPA made by §1089 of the Dodd-Frank Act are codified at 15 U.S.C. §§1692k, 1692l, 1692m, and 1692o. The FTC and certain other agencies retained enforcement authority under 15 U.S.C. §1692l . Also, the FTC retained rulemaking authority over auto dealers pursuant to §1029 of the Dodd-Frank Act. Pursuant to §1024(c)(3) of the Dodd-Frank Act. The CFPB and the FTC concluded a Memorandum of Understanding to establish a framework for coordinating enforcement efforts, which is available at http://www.ftc.gov/os/2012/01/120123ftc-cfpb-mou.pdf, while the press release is available at http://www.ftc.gov/opa/2012/01/ftccfpb.shtm. Regulation F, the Fair Debt Collection Practices Act regulations, is set forth at 12 C.F.R. part 1006, and is part of the CFPB's regulations promulgated at 76 Fed. Reg. 78121 (2011).
For more information on the transfer of functions to the CFPB, see CFPB, *Streamlining Inherited Regulations*, 76 Fed. Reg. 75825 (2011); CFPB, *Identification of Enforceable Rules and Orders*, 76 Fed. Reg. 43569 (2011); CFPB, *Agencies Issue Statement to Clarify Supervisory and Enforcement Responsibilities For Federal Consumer Financial Laws,* at http://www.consumerfinance.gov/pressrelease/agencies-issue-statement-to-clarify-supervisory-and- enforcement-responsibilities-for-federal-consumer-financial-laws; CRS Report R41338, *The Dodd-Frank Wall Street Reform and Consumer Protection Act: Title X, The Consumer Financial Protection Bureau*, by David H. Carpenter; and CRS Report R42572, *The Consumer Financial Protection Bureau (CFPB): A Legal Analysis*, by David H. Carpenter. The FTC issued a report on its experiences administering and enforcing the FCRA, *Forty Years of Experience with the Fair Credit Reporting Act: An FTC Staff Report and Summary of Interpretations* (2011), while simultaneously rescinding its official staff interpretations in the Code of Federal Regulations, in anticipation of the transfer of certain

regulatory functions to the CFPB. The FTC's report and rescission are available at http://www.ftc.gov/opa/2011/07/fcra.shtm.

17 15 U.S.C. §1692l.

18 2013 Report, *supra* note 2, at 42. The Dodd-Frank Act, §1061(b)(5)(D), 124 Stat. 1037 (2010), requires the CFPB and FTC to coordinate regulatory efforts to avoid duplication or conflict regarding their respective authorities under the Dodd-Frank Act and the Federal Trade Commission Act, codified as amended at 15 U.S.C. §§41-58.

19 15 U.S.C. §1692c(a). For the purposes of this section, the term "consumer" includes the consumer's spouse, parent (if the consumer is a minor), guardian, executor, or administrator. *Id.* §1692c(d).

20 *Id.*

21 *Id.* §1692c(a)(2).

22 *Id.* §1692d(1). This list is not exhaustive.

23 *Id.* §1692d(2) and (5).

24 *Id.* §1692d(6).

25 *Id.* §1692c(c).

26 *Id.* §1692b.

27 *Id.*

28 *Id.* Third parties may be contacted more than once if the debt collector reasonably believes that the earlier response was erroneous or incomplete and that the person now has correct or complete location information. *Id.* §1692b(3).

29 *Id.* §1692d(3) and (4).

30 *Id.* §1692e. This list is not exhaustive.

31 *Id.*

32 *Id.* §1692f. This list is not exhaustive.

33 *Id.* §1692g(a).

34 *Id.* §1692g(d) and (e).

35 *Id.* §1692g(b).

36 *Id.* §1692h.

37 *Id.* §1692k(a). Calculation of damages in a class action suit varies. *See* Id. §1692k(a)(2)(B).

38 *Id.* §1692k(b). A debt collector may not be held liable for a violation of the act, if he is able to show by a "preponderance of the evidence that the violation was not intentional and resulted from a bona fide error notwithstanding the maintenance of procedures reasonably adapted to avoid any such error." *Id.* §1692k(c).

39 *Id.* §1692l.

40 *See supra* notes 16, 17, and 18 and accompanying text.

41 *Id.*

42 12 U.S.C. §5514(a) and (e).

43 *Id.* at §5514(a).

44 77 Fed. Reg. 65775 (2012). The rule is codified at 12 C.F.R. §1090.105.

45 *Id.* at 65777 and 2013 Report, *supra* note 2, at 23.

46 2013 Report, *supra* note 2, at 23.

47 *Id.* at 65776.

48 *Id.* at 65783, noting authority under 12 U.S.C. §5515.

49 *Id.* at 65784-65785.

50 *Id.*

51 2013 Report, *supra* note 2, at 24. The CFPB describes the examination procedures on its website at http://www.consumerfinance.gov/pressreleases/consumer-financial-protection-bureau-to-oversee-debt-collectors as follows:

- Provide Required Disclosures: Examiners will evaluate whether debt collectors are properly identifying themselves and properly disclosing the amount of debt owed. The CFPB intends to ensure that debt collectors are upfront and clear with consumers.

- Provide Accurate Information: Examiners will assess whether debt collectors are using accurate data in their pursuit of debt. Inaccurate information can lead to collectors attempting to collect debt that consumers do not owe or have already paid.
- Have a Consumer Complaint and Dispute Resolution Process: As part of the CFPB's compliance management review, examiners will assess whether complaints are resolved adequately and in a timely manner, whether the complaints highlight violations of federal consumer financial law, and whether the debt collector has a process in place to address consumer disputes.
- Communicate Civilly and Honestly with Consumers: Examiners will be assessing whether debt collectors have harassed or deceived consumers in pursuit of debt. For example, debt collectors should not be using obscene or profane language with consumers. Nor should they be engaging the consumer in telephone conversations repeatedly or continuously with intent to annoy, abuse, or harass. Debt collectors cannot threaten to imprison consumers who do not pay their debt or threaten to tell the consumer's employer about the debt.

[52] FTC, *The Structure and Practices of the Debt Buying Industry* (2013) [*hereinafter* FTC Report], available at http://www.ftc.gov/os/2013/01/debtbuyingreport.pdf.
[53] *Id.* at i-ii.
[54] *Id.* at ii.
[55] *Id.*
[56] *Id.* at iv.
[57] *Id.*
[58] *Id.* at ii-iii
[59] *Id.*
[60] *Id.*
[61] *Id.* at iv-v.
[62] *Id.*
[63] *Id.* at 49.
[64] *Id.*
[65] 2013 Report, *supra* note 2, at 41.
[66] *Id.* and FTC, Final Transcript of *Debt Collection 2.0: Protecting Consumers as Technologies Change* [*hereinafter* Final Transcript], available at http://www.ftc.gov/bcp/workshops/debtcollectiontech/docs/transcript.pdf.
[67] *Id.*
[68] *See supra* notes 16, 17, and 18 and accompanying text regarding regulatory and supervisory functions of the CFPB and shared enforcement authorities and memorandum of understanding for coordination of enforcement efforts regarding the debt collection market.
[69] 15 U.S.C. §1692l.
[70] P.L. 111-203, title X, §1031, 124 Stat. 2005 (2010), codified as amended at 15 U.S.C. §5531.
[71] FTCA §5, codified as amended at 15 U.S.C. §45.
[72] 2013 Report, *supra* note 2, at 25-34.
[73] *Id.* at 12-21. The complaints are classified generally as harassing the alleged debtor or others; demanding an amount other than is permitted by law or contract; failing to send required written notice of the debt to consumer; threatening dire consequences if consumer fails to pay; failing to identify self as a debt collector; revealing alleged debt to third parties; impermissible calls to consumer's place of employment; failing to verify disputed debts; and continuing to contact consumer after receiving "cease communication." *Id. See also* **Figure 1**, on FDCPA complaint type, number, and percentage in 2012 and 2011, and **Figure 2**, on number of complaints received in each debt collection practice category, 2008–2012, *infra* at 13-14, reprinted from the 2013 Report, *supra* note 2, at 16 and 57, respectively.
[74] 2013 Report, *supra* note 2, at 12-13.
[75] *Id.* at 12-13.

[76] *Id.*
[77] Dodd-Frank Act, P.L. 111-203, title X, §1034, 124 Stat. 2008 (2010), codified at 12 U.S.C. §5534.
[78] *Id.* at 11-12.
[79] 2013 Report, *supra* note 2, at 27-28.
[80] *Id.*
[81] *Id.*
[82] *Id.*
[83] *Id.*
[84] *Id.*
[85] *Id.*
[86] *Id.*
[87] *Id.* at 28.
[88] *Id.*
[89] *Id.* at 28-34.
[90] *Id.*
[91] *Id.* at 32.
[92] ______ U.S. ______, 133 S. Ct. 1166; 185 L. Ed. 2d 242 (2013).
[93] 2013 Report, *supra* note 2, at 26.
[94] *Id.* at 32-33 and Brief for the United States as Amicus Curiae Supporting Petitioner, 2011 U.S. Briefs 1175, 2012 U.S. S. Ct. Briefs LEXIS 3149 (August 3, 2012).
[95] *Id.*
[96] As noted above, the exclusion of first-party debt collectors from FDCPA coverage is partly mitigated by CFPB and FTC Dodd-Frank and FTCA authority.
[97] See Michael D. Slodov, *Documentation? I Don't Have To Show You Any Stinkin' Documentation! An Evaluation of the Verification Requirement of 15 U.S.C. § 1692g(B)*, 24 Loy. Consumer L. Rev. 156 (2011), discussing the two interpretations of the FDCPA validation requirement as requiring a double-check verification or actual investigation of the substantive information for a debt; Mary Spector, *Debts, Defaults and Details: Exploring the Impact of Debt Collection Litigation on Consumers and Courts*, 6 Va. L. & Bus. Rev. 257, 261, 298 (2011), describing inadequate information and/or debt verification provided to consumers, including alleged robo-signing of affidavits documenting or verifying debts. *See also* Congressional Research Service Legal Sidebar, *Robo-Signing Rerun, This Time Involving Credit Cards?*by David H. Carpenter, available at http://www.crs.gov/analysis/legalsidebar/pages/details.aspx?ProdId= 202.
[98] Richard M. Alderman, *The Fair Debt Collection Practices Act Meets Arbitration: Non-Parties and Arbitration*, 24 Loy. Consumer L. Rev. 586 (2012), discussing the potential of arbitration clauses between a creditor and debtor to limit a debtor's ability to litigate legal violations related to debt collection against third-party debt collector and to limit class actions.
[99] Eileen Ambrose, *Activists decry 'debtors prisons,' but others call it justice*, Chicago Tribune, C1 (April 4, 2013); Jim Gallagher, *Creditors use police, courts to harry debtors Illinois restricts 'body attachment' for civil debt; practice has little public opposition in Missouri*, St. Louis Post-Dispatch, A1 (Aug. 19, 2012); Jessica Silver-Greenberg, *Debtor Arrests Criticized*, Wall Street Journal, C3 (Nov. 22, 2011).
[100] See Laurie A. Lucas, Tomio B. Narita, and Anna-Katrina S. Christakis, *Recent Cases Concerning the Treatment of Attorney Debt Collectors Under the FDCPA*, 66 Bus. Law. 551 (2011), discussing the limitations on the bona-fide error defense after *Jerman v. Carlisle, McNellie, Rini, Kramer & Ulrich, L.P.A.*, 559 U.S. 573, 130 S. Ct. 1605 (2010), in which the U.S. Supreme Court held that the bona-fide error defense for the FDCPA under 15 U.S.C. §1692k(c) does not apply to a violation resulting from a debt collector's error in interpreting FDCPA requirements.

[101] Bruce Menkes and Anna-Katrina S. Christakis, *Fair Debt Collections Update: Communications and Other Issues*, 64 Bus. Law. 665 (2009), discussing *Foti v. NCO Fin. Sys., Inc.*, 424 F. Supp. 2d 643 (S.D.N.Y. 2006) (court held that a standard pre-recorded message left at the consumer's home as a follow-up to a validation notice was a communication under the FDCPA that violated the FDCPA by failing to meet requirements for a communication). *See also* Final Transcript, *supra* note 66, mentioning *Foti*-related concerns regarding use of telephone technology in debt collections.

[102] S. 508, Strengthen and Vitalize Enforcement of Child Support (SAVE Child Support) Act, amends the FDCPA to cover a debt arising from a child support order; it excludes from the definition of "debt collector" any private child support collection agency licensed by a state to collect support obligations under the state plan for child and spousal support pursuant to the Social Security Act.

[103] H.R. 2361, 112th Cong (2011).

[104] S. 3350, 112th Cong. (2012).

[105] H.R. 1783, 112th Cong. (2012); S. 824, 112th Cong. (2012).

[106] H.R. 4101, 112th Cong. (2012), and H.R. 5794, 112th Cong. (2012).

In: Fair Debt Collection Practices Act
Editor: Sven De Boer
ISBN: 978-1-62808-116-9

Chapter 2

FAIR DEBT COLLECTION PRACTICES ACT: CFPB ANNUAL REPORT 2013*

Consumer Financial Protection Bureau

1. INTRODUCTION

The Consumer Financial Protection Bureau ("CFPB" or "the Bureau") is pleased to submit to Congress its second annual report summarizing its activities to administer the Fair Debt Collection Practices Act ("FDCPA" or "the Act"), 15 U.S.C. §§ 1692 *et seq.*, during the past year. These activities represent the Bureau's efforts to curtail deceptive, unfair, and abusive debt collection practices in the marketplace.

Last year the Bureau issued its inaugural annual report to Congress, following the Dodd-Frank Act's transfer of responsibility from the Federal Trade Commission ("FTC") to the Bureau.[1] The FTC had previously prepared this report annually since the FDCPA's enactment in 1977. Under the Dodd-Frank Act, the Bureau has primary government responsibility for administering the FDCPA. The Bureau has the authority to prescribe rules with respect to debt collection; issue guidance concerning compliance with the law; collect complaint data; educate consumers and collectors; and undertake research and policy initiatives related to consumer debt collection.[2] The

* This is an edited, reformatted and augmented version of the Consumer Financial Protection Bureau, dated March 20, 2013.

Bureau shares overall enforcement responsibility with the FTC and other federal agencies.

Over the past year, the Bureau and the FTC have continued to collaborate in the area of debt collection. Consistent with those efforts, the FTC has provided the Bureau with a letter summarizing its debt collection activities during the past year. As in previous years, the FTC took significant steps in 2012 to curtail illegal debt collection practices. Information about the FTC's activities is incorporated into this report, and the FTC's letter is included in this report as Appendix A.[3] The Bureau is grateful to the FTC for its assistance with this annual report.

This report (1) provides background on the FDCPA and the debt collection market; (2) summarizes the Bureau's Consumer Response function and the number and types of consumer complaints regarding debt collection received by the FTC in 2012; (3) describes the Bureau's supervision program as it relates to debt collection; (4) presents recent developments in the Bureau and FTC's law enforcement and advocacy programs; (5) discusses recent education and outreach initiatives; (6) discusses recent research and policy initiatives; and (7) discusses coordination and cooperation between the Bureau and the FTC in the administration of the FDCPA.

2. BACKGROUND

Debt collection is a large, multi-billion dollar industry that directly impacts many consumers. In 2012, approximately 30 million individuals, or 14% of American adults, had debt that was or had been subject to the collections process (averaging approximately $1,500.[4] Many Americans, including consumer populations identified in the Dodd-Frank Act—students, older Americans, servicemembers and veterans—were hit hard by the recession and are increasingly challenged by debt in collections. After finding "abundant evidence of the use of abusive, deceptive, and unfair debt collection practices by many debt collectors,"[5] Congress passed the FDCPA in 1977 to eliminate abusive collection practices by debt collectors and to ensure that those debt collectors who refrain from using abusive practices are not competitively disadvantaged. Congress also found that "[a]busive debt collection practices contribute to the number of personal bankruptcies, to marital instability, to the loss of jobs, and to invasions of individual privacy."[6] The FDCPA created important parameters on debt collection activities such as the time and place collection calls could be made, restrictions on how and to whom debts are communicated, and prohibitions on deceptive, threatening, and abusive collection tactics. The FDCPA principally applies only to third-party collectors; in general these are collection agencies, debt purchasers, and attorneys regularly engaging in debt collection. For the most part, first-party creditors are not subject to the FDCPA, although the Dodd-Frank Act, state laws, and Section 5 of the FTC Act prohibit them from engaging in unfair, deceptive or abusive practices in their own collection activity. Both the CFPB and the FTC have law enforcement powers under the FDCPA.

Today's collection industry is markedly different from the industry contemplated when Congress enacted the FDCPA 36 years ago. Since the FDCPA's enactment, debt purchasing has emerged as a major industry. Debt buyers buy (and sometimes sell) distressed consumer debt in an attempt to liquidate charged-off creditor receivables. The DBA International, an industry association for debt buyers, reports approximately 600 association members. The vast majority of these firms did not exist when Congress passed the FDCPA, and those that existed were not engaged in the large-scale debt purchasing that occurs today. In addition, collectors more commonly use litigation as a collection strategy than they did when the FDCPA was enacted.

Furthermore, evolving technology has significantly impacted the collections industry. Banks and financial institutions use advanced information and credit risk models to extend credit to Americans who might not have received it 36 years ago. Technology has also helped the industry respond to increasing numbers of consumers with delinquent debt payments. Once, collection activities depended on typewritten collection notices and local phone calls, and virtually everyone subject to collection efforts received a call or a letter. Today, both creditors and collection firms may use sophisticated analytics to identify specific debtors to target. This reduces calls and letters to consumers who are most likely to pay without prompting. Automated dialers, predictive dialing algorithms, and internet telephony have lowered the cost of contacting consumers for collection firms.

Consumer debt collection plays an important role in the functioning of the consumer credit market. By collecting delinquent debt, collectors reduce creditors' losses from non-repayment and thereby may help to keep consumer credit available and more affordable to consumers. In some instances, by purchasing debt at discounted rates, debt buyers may be able to offer consumers settlements and payment plans that original creditors would be unlikely to offer, making it easier for consumers to pay off their debts. Available and affordable credit is vital to millions of consumers because it makes it possible for them to purchase goods and services that they could not afford if they had to pay the entire cost at the time of purchase.

Even as the industry has changed, abuses still exist and the industry remains a top source of consumer complaints. There is still a need to protect consumers from debt collectors who violate the FDCPA, or who engage in deceptive, unfair, or abusive collection practices. These practices are not only illegal, but they can also adversely affect a consumer's employment and ability to repay the debt. Also, debt collectors who refrain from using unlawful debt collection practices should not be competitively disadvantaged.

3. Consumer Complaints

3.1. The Bureau's Consumer Response

Collecting, investigating, and responding to consumer complaints are integral parts of the CFPB's work, as Congress set forth in the Dodd-Frank Act. [7] The Office of Consumer Response "Consumer Response" hears directly from consumers about the challenges they face in the marketplace, reviews consumer complaints, and brings those concerns to the attention of companies.

Consumer Response began operations on July 21, 2011, accepting consumer complaints about credit cards. Next, it accepted mortgage complaints beginning on December 1, 2011, followed on March 1, 2012, by complaints about bank accounts and services, private student loans, and consumer loans. Most recently, on October 22, 2012, Consumer Response began handling credit-reporting complaints. The CFPB continues to work towards expanding its complaint handling to include other products and services under its authority, including debt collection.

The CFPB accepts consumer complaints through its website and by telephone, mail, email, fax, and referral. Consumers file complaints on the Bureau's website using complaint forms tailored to specific products and can also log on to a secure consumer portal to check the status of a complaint and review a company's response. While on the website, consumers can chat with a live agent to receive help completing a complaint form. Consumers can also call the Bureau's toll-free number to ask questions, file a complaint, check the status of a complaint, and more.

The CFPB's U.S.-based contact centers handle calls with little-to-no wait times. The contact centers provide services to consumers in more than 180 languages, and to hearing- and speech- impaired consumers via a toll-free telephone number. Cutting-edge technology, including secure company and consumer portals, makes the process safe, efficient, and user-friendly for consumers and companies.

The FTC, which accepts complaints regarding debt collection through its Consumer Sentinel database, has provided to the Bureau the following data on consumer complaints regarding debt collection submitted to the FTC in 2012.

3.2. Consumer Complaints Submitted to the FTC

The FTC receives information about the conduct of debt collectors from complaints consumers file with the FTC and from its enforcement work.[8] The FTC uses consumer complaints generally to monitor the industry, select targets, and conduct preliminary analysis that, with further factual development, might reveal or help prove a law violation.

Based on the FTC's experience, many consumers never file complaints with anyone other than the debt collector itself. Other consumers complain only to the underlying creditor or to enforcement agencies other than the FTC. Some consumers may not be aware that the conduct they have experienced violates the FDCPA or that the FTC enforces the FDCPA. For these reasons, the total number of consumer complaints the FTC receives may understate the extent to which the practices of debt collectors violate the law.

On the other hand, the FTC acknowledges that not all of the debt collection practices about which consumers complain necessarily comprise legal violations. Many consumers complain of conduct that, if accurately described, would indeed violate the FDCPA, or Section 5 of the Federal Trade Commission Act ("FTC Act"), 15 U.S.C. § 45. The FTC, however, does not verify whether the information consumers provide is accurate unless the agency undertakes such an inquiry in connection with its law enforcement activities. Moreover, even if accurately described, some conduct about which consumers complain does not violate the FDCPA. And, in some cases, consumers may complain of conduct about which more information is needed to determine whether it would violate the law.

Despite these limitations, the FTC continues to believe that consumer complaint data provides useful insight into the acts and practices of debt collectors. Below is a description of trends that the FTC has observed in the overall number of debt collection complaints it has received as well as the types of practices about which consumers complain most frequently. The total number of FTC complaints, as well as the number of complaints reported to the FTC about any specific practice, fluctuates yearly for a variety of reasons. To convey the relative impact of a particular practice on consumers during the past year, this report presents the percentage of all 2012 FTC complaints related to each specific practice. To assist in identifying trends over time, this report compares the percentage of all FDCPA complaints to the FTC in 2012 pertinent to a practice with the percentage of all such complaints in 2011 that pertain to the same practice.

3.2.1. Total Number of FTC Complaints[9]

Hundreds of thousands of consumers contact the FTC every year about consumer protection issues. With respect to debt collection, the FTC receives both consumer inquiries and complaints. The FTC's Consumer Response Center ("CRC") makes every effort to distinguish between these two categories of contacts. The data presented here include only consumer contacts that the CRC has identified as complaints.[10] When this section of the report references "complaints," it includes only complaints that consumers have filed directly with the FTC, as opposed to any other body.[11]

All Collectors

The FTC continues to receive more complaints about the debt collection industry than any other specific industry.[12] However, the number of complaints related to the industry that were filed directly with the FTC declined in 2012 as compared to 2011.[13]

Complaints about third-party debt collectors[14] and in-house collectors in 2012 together totaled 125,136 complaints[15] and accounted for 24.1% of all complaints the FTC received.[16]

This represents a 13.4% decrease in absolute terms and a 3.4% decrease as a percentage of total complaints over 2011, when the agency received 144,451 debt collection complaints, accounting for 27.5% of all complaints the FTC received.

Third-Party Debt Collectors

In 2012, consumer complaints to the FTC about third-party debt collectors ("FDCPA complaints") decreased in absolute terms by 13.6%, and as a percentage of all complaints that consumers filed directly with the FTC. The FTC received 102,783 FDCPA complaints in 2012, representing 19.8% of all complaints it received directly from consumers. By comparison, in 2011, the FTC received 118,945 FDCPA complaints, representing 22.6% of the complaints it received directly from consumers.

In-House Debt Collectors

Last year, the number of complaints the FTC received about creditors' in-house collectors decreased slightly, both in absolute terms and as a percentage of total complaints. In 2012, the FTC received 22,353 complaints about in-house collectors, representing 4.3% of all complaints received. In 2011, the FTC received 25,506 complaints about in-house collectors, representing 4.9% of all complaints received.

Although the FTC received over 100,000 consumer complaints about third-party collectors in 2012, it recognizes that collectors contact millions of consumers each year. The number of complaints the FTC receives about debt collectors, therefore, corresponds to only a small fraction of the overall number of consumers contacted.

3.2.2. FTC Complaints by Category

In addition to evaluating the total number of complaints about third-party debt collectors, it also is instructive to consider the specific types of debt collection practices about which consumers complain. Because consumer complaints frequently address more than one debt collection practice, the complaint may have been assigned many more than one code by the FTC's CRC.[17] Thus, if one adds together all the complaints for each of the fifteen debt collection codes each year, the total exceeds the number of FDCPA complaints the FTC actually received in that year.[18]

The following graph compares the number of complaints received in each debt collection practice category from 2008 through 2012.

Harassing the Alleged Debtor or Others

This complaint category encompasses four distinct violation codes. Under the FDCPA, debt collectors may not harass consumers to try to collect on a debt.[19]

In 2012, 36.5% of FDCPA complaints the FTC received, or 37,543 complaints, claimed that collectors harassed the complainants by calling repeatedly or continuously. This represents a reduction of 21% from 2011. This was the second most frequent law violation about which consumers complained during 2012, down from first in 2011, when 47,573 FDCPA complaints, representing 40.0% of FDCPA complaints, stated that collectors harassed them by calling repeatedly or continuously.

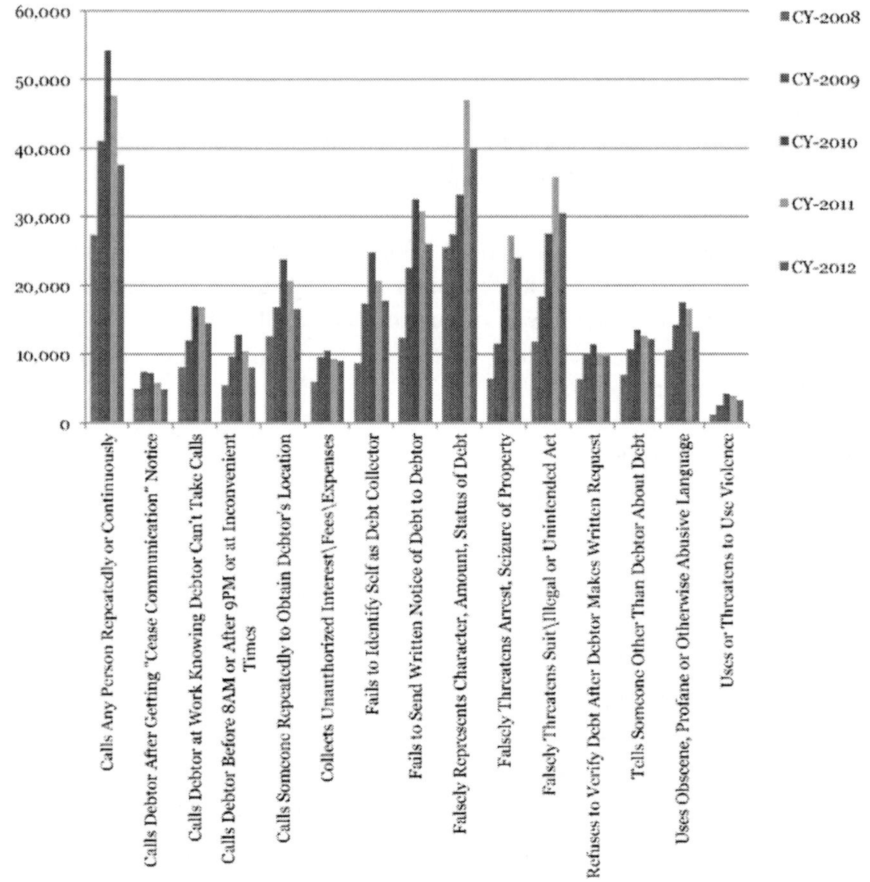

Also in 2012, 13.0% of FDCPA complaints, or 13,329 complaints, claimed that a collector had used obscene, profane, or abusive language. In 2011, 14.0% of FDCPA complaints, or 16,610 complaints, raised concerns about this practice. Allegations that collectors called before 8:00 a.m., after 9:00 p.m., or at other times that the collectors knew or should have known were inconvenient to the consumer, made up 7.9% of complaints, or 8,166 complaints, in 2012, down from 8.8% of complaints, or 10,494 complaints, in 2011. Reports that collectors used or threatened to use violence if consumers failed to pay accounted for 3.2% of FDCPA complaints in 2012, or 3,312 complaints, down from 3.3% of complaints, or 3,980 complaints, in 2011.

Demanding an Amount Other than is Permitted by Law or Contract

This category includes two different FDCPA law violation codes. First, the FDCPA prohibits debt collectors from misrepresenting the character, amount, or legal status of a debt.[20] The types of complaints that fall into this category, for example, are reports that a debt collector is attempting to collect either a debt the consumer does not owe at all or a debt larger than what the consumer actually owes. Other complaints in this category state that collectors are seeking to collect on debts that have been discharged in bankruptcy. For the first time in five years, this is the most common category of FDCPA complaint, up from the second most common category. In 2012, there were 39,993 complaints describing this conduct, representing 38.9% of FDCPA complaints. In 2011, this category accounted for 47,012 complaints, or 39.5%.

Second, the FDCPA prohibits debt collectors from collecting any amount unless it is "expressly authorized by the agreement creating the debt or permitted by law."[21] In 2012, 8.8% of FDCPA complaints, or 9,034 complaints, asserted that collectors demanded interest, fees, or expenses that were not owed (such as unauthorized collection fees, late fees, and court costs). In 2011, 7.8% of FDCPA complaints, or 9,325, made these assertions.

Failing to Send Required Written Notice of the Debt to Consumer

The FDCPA requires that debt collectors send consumers a written notice that includes, among other things, the amount of the debt, the name of the creditor to whom the debt is owed, and a statement that, if within thirty days of receiving the notice the consumer disputes the debt in writing, the collector will obtain verification of the debt and mail it to the consumer.[22] Many consumers who do not receive this notice are unaware that they must dispute their debts in writing if they wish to obtain verification of the debts. In 2012, 25.4%, of the FDCPA complaints, or 26,139 complaints, reported that collectors did not provide the required notice, slightly down from 25.9% of all FDCPA complaints, or 30,753 complaints, in 2011.

Threatening Dire Consequences If Consumer Fails to Pay

The FDCPA bars debt collectors from making threats as to what might happen if the consumer fails to pay the debt, unless the collector has the legal authority and the intent to take the threatened action.[23] Among other things, collectors might threaten to initiate civil suit or criminal prosecution, garnish wages, seize property, cause loss of job, have a consumer jailed, or damage or ruin a consumer's credit rating. In 2012, 29.6% of FDCPA complaints, or 30,470 complaints, reported that third-party collectors falsely threatened a lawsuit or some other action that they could not or did not intend to take, a slight decrease from the 30.0% of FDCPA complaints, or 35,738 complaints that reported the same type of conduct in 2011. Also in 2012, 23.4% of FDCPA complaints, or 24,062 complaints, alleged that such collectors falsely threatened arrest or seizure of property. This number is up as an overall percentage, but down in absolute terms, from 2011, when 22.9% of FDCPA complaints, or 27,270 complaints, reported such conduct.

Failing to Identify Self as a Debt Collector

To avoid creating a false or misleading impression, the FDCPA requires a debt collector to disclose in all communications with a consumer that he or she is a debt collector and, in the first communication with the consumer, that he or she is attempting to collect a debt and that any information obtained will be used for that purpose.[24] Consumers who do not receive such notification may reveal under false pretenses information that will later be used against them to collect the alleged debt. In 2012, 17.4% of all FDCPA complaints, or 17,873 complaints, alleged the collector failed to provide the required "mini-Miranda" warning, down slightly from 17.5% of FDCPA complaints, or 20,793 complaints, in 2011.

Revealing Alleged Debt to Third Parties

The FDCPA generally prohibits third-party contacts for any purpose other than obtaining information about the consumer's location.[25] Collectors calling to obtain location information also are prohibited from revealing that a consumer allegedly owes a debt.[26]

Improper third-party contacts may embarrass or intimidate the consumer who allegedly owes the debt and be a continuing aggravation to the third parties. In some cases, collectors reportedly have made misrepresentations as well as used harassing and abusive tactics in their communications with third parties, or even have attempted to collect from the third party.

Contacts with consumers' employers and co-workers about consumers' alleged debts also may jeopardize continued employment or prospects for promotion. Relationships between consumers and their families, friends, or neighbors may additionally suffer from improper third-party contacts.

This past year, 16.2% of FDCPA complaints, or 16,679 complaints, claimed that collectors called a third party repeatedly to obtain location information about the consumer,[27] down from 17.5% of complaints, or 20,798 complaints, in 2011. The third parties contacted included employers, relatives, children, neighbors, and friends. Also in 2012, 11.9% of all FDCPA complaints, or 12,272 complaints, reported that debt collectors illegally disclosed a purported debt to a third party. This number was up as a percentage, but down in absolute terms, as compared to 2011, when 10.6% of FDCPA complaints, or 12,654 complaints, reported these disclosures.

Impermissible Calls to Consumer's Place of Employment

Under the FDCPA, a debt collector may not contact a consumer at work if the collector knows or has reason to know that the consumer's employer prohibits such contacts.[28] By continuing to contact consumers at work under these circumstances, debt collectors may put them in jeopardy of losing their jobs. In 2012, 14.1% of FDCPA complaints, or 14,482 complaints, related to calls to consumers at work, down from 14.2% of FDCPA complaints, or 16,932 complaints, in 2011.

Failing to Verify Disputed Debts

The FDCPA also mandates that, if a consumer submits a dispute in writing, the collector must cease collection efforts until it has provided written verification of the debt.[29] Many consumers complained that collectors ignored their written disputes, sent no verification, and continued their collection efforts. Other consumers reported that some collectors continued to contact them about the debts between the date the consumers submitted their dispute and the date the collectors provided the verification. Last year, 9.5% of all FDCPA complaints, or 9,814 complaints, claimed that collectors failed to verify disputed debts. In 2011, 8.4% of all FDCPA complaints, or 10,002 complaints, were of this type.

Continuing to Contact Consumer after Receiving "Cease Communication"

The FDCPA requires debt collectors to cease all communications with a consumer about an alleged debt if the consumer communicates in writing that he or she wants all such communications to stop or that he or she refuses to pay the alleged debt.[30] This "cease communication" notice does not prevent collectors or creditors from filing suit against the consumer to collect, but it does prohibit collectors from calling the consumer or sending further notices. In 2012, 4.8% of FDCPA complaints, or 4,928 complaints, reported that collectors ignored "cease communication" notices and continued their collection attempts, down from 5.0% of complaints, or 5,933 complaints, in 2011.

4. Bureau Supervision of Debt Collection Activities

4.1. Final Rulemaking: "Larger Participants" of the Consumer Debt Collection Market

Under the Dodd-Frank Act, the Bureau has the authority to supervise certain nonbank entities that offer or provide consumer financial products or services. Specifically, the Bureau has authority to supervise nonbank entities in the residential mortgage, payday lending, and private education lending markets. This authority extends to these entities' service providers, including third-party debt collectors.[31] In addition, for other nonbank markets for consumer financial products or services, the Bureau has the authority to supervise "larger participants" under Section 1024(a)(1)(B) as the Bureau defines by rule.

On October 31, 2012, the CFPB published a final rule defining "larger participants" in the consumer debt collection market, which became effective on January 2, 2013.[32] When it announced the larger participant rule for debt collection, the Bureau held a field hearing on debt collection in Seattle, WA. The field hearing provided the Bureau an opportunity to get valuable input from various stakeholders. Participants included industry, consumer groups, and individual consumers who spoke about debt collection issues they faced.

The final rule establishes the first federal supervision program for the debt collection industry, bringing debt collectors with more than $10 million in annual receipts resulting from consumer debt collection within the scope of the CFPB's supervisory authority. Based on available data, the Bureau estimates that the rule covers approximately 175 debt collection firms—or 4% of debt collection firms—and that these firms account for 63% of annual receipts from the debt collection market. The market covered by the rule includes three main types of consumer debt collectors: firms that buy defaulted debt and collect the proceeds for themselves, firms that collect defaulted debt owned by another company in return for a fee, and debt collection attorneys. The Bureau will examine consumer debt collectors on a risk basis to ensure that they comply with statutory and regulatory requirements related to the Federal consumer financial laws. Ensuring compliance with the FDCPA will be central to all examinations of debt collectors.

4.2. Debt Collection Supervision Program

Under the Dodd-Frank Act, the Bureau has the authority to supervise many creditors who collect their own debts or hire third-party debt collectors, their service providers for collection services, and, now that the "larger participant" rule is in effect, larger nonbank debt collectors. For the first time, a single federal agency supervises creditors and third-party debt collection firms and debt buyers. As such, the Bureau is in a position to evaluate whether federal consumer laws are being followed at every stage of the lending process–from credit origination to debt collection.

On October 24, 2012, the Bureau released its *Debt Collection Examination Procedures,* which are an extension of the Bureau's general *Supervisory and Examination Manual.*[33] *The Debt Collection Examination Procedures* provide guidance on how the Bureau will be conducting its monitoring of both banks and nonbanks engaging in consumer debt collection. Examiners will evaluate the quality of the entity's compliance-management systems, review practices to ensure they comply with Federal consumer financial laws, and identify risks to consumers throughout the debt collection process. The Bureau has issued similar procedures for other companies under its supervision, such as consumer reporting agencies, mortgage originators, mortgage servicers, and payday lenders.

The Bureau takes confidentiality of company information very seriously. Consistent with the policies of the prudential regulators, the Bureau's policy is to treat information obtained in the supervisory process as confidential and privileged.[34]

5. ENFORCEMENT

5.1. Bureau Enforcement and Advocacy

5.1.1. Bureau Enforcement

In October 2012, the Bureau announced its first public enforcement action involving debt collection practices. The Bureau required three American Express subsidiaries to refund an estimated $85 million to approximately 250,000 customers for several distinct illegal card practices, including deceptive debt collection. Because American Express was engaged in first-party debt collection activities, the debt collection claims relied upon the Dodd-Frank Act rather than the FDCPA. The Bureau, along with the Federal

Deposit Insurance Corporation ("FDIC"), Office of the Comptroller of the Currency, and the Federal Reserve Board, found that subsidiaries of American Express deceived consumers regarding certain benefits to paying off old debt.

American Express wrongly told consumers that if they paid off the old debt, the payment would be reported to credit bureaus and could improve their credit scores. In fact, American Express was not reporting the payments and the debt was so old that even if they had tried to report them, many of the payments would not have appeared on these consumers' credit reports or affected their credit scores. American Express also told some consumers that a portion of their debt would be waived or forgiven if they accepted certain settlement offers when in fact, the debt was not forgiven if they applied for a new card with American Express.

As a result of the enforcement actions, American Express was ordered to provide full restitution, plus interest, to all consumers who were wrongly told that it would report payment to credit bureaus. American Express was also ordered to provide $100 and a pre-approved offer for a new card, with terms the CFPB and FDIC find acceptable, to each consumer who accepted the deceptive debt settlement offer and was then denied a new card because the debt was not forgiven. Consumers who already paid the waived or forgiven amount are being refunded that amount, plus interest. American Express was also ordered to reform its debt collection practices and to notify consumers when collecting older debt that can no longer be the subject of litigation or credit reporting.

Going forward, American Express is prohibited from collecting debt when it lacks adequate documentation evidencing the debt. At a minimum, this documentation must include consumer agreements and amendments and a complete transactional history of the debt. The Bureau also assessed civil money penalties totaling $14.1 million against American Express for its deceptive debt collection practices and other violations of consumer financial protection laws.

In addition to the Bureau's first public enforcement action involving debt collection practices, the Bureau is also conducting several non-public investigations of companies to determine whether they engaged in collection practices that violate the FDCPA or the Dodd-Frank Act.

5.1.2. Bureau Advocacy on Behalf Of Consumers

In the past year, the Bureau has appeared as an amicus (friend of the court) in two cases arising under the FDCPA. In one, the Bureau presented oral argument in the 11th Circuit Court of Appeals and in the other, the Bureau joined the Solicitor General and the FTC in filing a brief in the U.S. Supreme Court.

Marx v. General Revenue Corp.

As discussed in last year's report, in January 2012, the Bureau filed an amicus brief in this case in the Tenth Circuit Court of Appeals urging the court to rehear a three-judge panel's decision that the Bureau argued eroded two important FDCPA protections—the general ban on contacting third parties in connection with debt collection and the FDCPA's limitation on good- faith plaintiffs' liability for a defendant's costs. As noted last year, the court declined to rehear the case. But in May 2012, the Supreme Court agreed to hear the question relating to plaintiffs' liability for a defendant's costs.

In August 2012, the Bureau and the FTC joined the Solicitor General's Office in filing an amicus brief in the Supreme Court, arguing that a consumer who loses a suit under the FDCPA does not have to pay the defendant's court costs unless she filed the suit in bad faith and for the purpose of harassment. On February 26, 2013, the Supreme Court issued a decision disagreeing with the government's position.

This case concerned the interaction of the FDCPA's provision on costs and the Federal Rule of Civil Procedure's default rule on costs. Federal Rule of Civil Procedure 54(d) authorizes a district court to award costs to the prevailing party "[u]nless a federal statute . . . provides otherwise." In a 7-2 decision, the Supreme Court held that the FDCPA did not "provide[] otherwise" than Rule 54(d). The relevant FDCPA provision specifies that "[o]n a finding by the court that an action under this section was brought in bad faith and for the purpose of harassment, the court may award to the defendant attorney's fees reasonable in relation to the work expended and costs." 15 U.S.C. § 1692k(a)(3). The Court held that this provision did not "provide[] otherwise" than Rule 54(d) because, in light of its context, it did not carry the negative implication that costs can be awarded to a prevailing defendant *only* if the plaintiff sued in bad faith. Rule 54(d) therefore applies in FDCPA actions and allows prevailing defendants to recover their costs from plaintiffs without a showing of bad faith. A more extensive description of the facts and legal arguments presented in Marx is set forth by the FTC in Section 5.2.3a below.

Paul and Angela Birster v. American Home Mortgage Servicing, Inc. (11th Cir.)

As discussed in last year's report, the Bureau filed an amicus brief in this case in December 2011. The Bureau appeared as amicus curiae in the oral argument in the case in May 2012. The case concerned FDCPA coverage in the foreclosure context—an important issue on which the federal district courts have been divided.

Some courts have unduly restricted the FDCPA's protections by rejecting challenges to harmful practices occurring in the context of foreclosure proceedings. In particular, courts have concluded that businesses involved in enforcing security interests are not "debt collectors" subject to most of the Act's requirements, and that activity surrounding foreclosure or other enforcement of security interests is not debt collection covered by the Act. These decisions have left consumers vulnerable to harmful collection tactics as they fight to save their homes from foreclosure.

In this FDCPA action, two consumers brought suit under the FDCPA against a company alleged to have repeatedly made harassing and threatening phone calls to induce the consumers to pay their mortgage debt to avoid foreclosure. The district court rejected the consumers' claims on the ground that the company was also pursuing foreclosure, and thus that the challenged practices related to enforcement of a security interest, which does not qualify as "debt collection" under the Act. The consumers appealed. The appeal presented the questions (1) whether an entity that satisfies the Act's general definition of "debt collector" is subject to the entire Act even though its principal purpose is the enforcement of security interests and (2) whether conduct related to enforcement of a security interest can also qualify as debt collection activity covered by the Act.

The Bureau's amicus brief explained that the district court erred when it concluded that the company did not qualify as a debt collector and that its actions in this case did not relate to debt collection.

On July 18, 2012, the Eleventh Circuit issued a decision agreeing with the Bureau's position.[35] That decision followed the court's May 2012 published decision in another case, *Reese v. Ellis, Painter, Ratterree & Adams, LLP,* 678 F.3d 1211 (11th Cir. 2012), in which the court made clear that (1) businesses involved in enforcing security interests can also constitute "debt collectors" subject to the entire FDCPA if they also regularly collect or attempt to collect debts, and (2) demanding payment of money qualifies as debt collection subject to the FDCPA even if the demands also relate to enforcement of a security interest. The Bureau did not file a brief in *Reese*—as briefing concluded before the Bureau's launch date—but the panel that decided that case had received the Bureau's *Birster* brief.

5.2. FTC Enforcement

As explained in the FTC letter, to improve deterrence in recent years, the FTC has focused on bringing a greater number of cases and obtaining stronger monetary and injunctive remedies against debt collectors that violate the law. Over the past year, the FTC has brought or resolved seven debt collection cases, matching the highest number of debt collection cases that it has brought or resolved in any single year. In each of its six Section 13(b) cases involving debt collection, the FTC obtained preliminary or permanent injunctive relief.[36] In many of these cases, the preliminary relief that was obtained included ex parte temporary restraining orders with asset freezes, immediate access to business premises, and appointment of receivers to run the debt collection business.

As discussed below, these cases represent an extensive and concerted effort by the FTC to target inappropriate debt collection practices that pose substantial risks to consumers. These practices include false threats, harassment or abuse, and attempts to collect on phantom payday loan debts.

5.2.1. Deceptive, Unfair and Abusive Collector Conduct

The FTC reports that one of its highest priorities is targeting debt collectors that engage in deceptive, unfair, or abusive conduct. In the past year, the FTC filed or resolved four actions in this area. In *FTC v. Forensic Case Management Services, Inc.,* after over a year of litigation, the FTC has secured substantial monetary judgments against a debt collection enterprise and a complete ban on future debt collection activity, along with other injunctive relief.[37] The FTC's complaint alleged that the defendants violated the FTC Act and the FDCPA through such egregious conduct as threatening to physically harm consumers and desecrate the bodies of their dead relatives; threatening to kill consumers' pets; using obscene and profane language; revealing consumers' debts to third parties; and falsely threatening consumers with lawsuits, arrest, and wage garnishment. The FTC entered into settlements with six individuals and three corporations responsible for the enterprise, as well as three relief defendants, for judgments totaling over $35.5 million.[38] The judgments were partially suspended based on the defendants' inability to pay, although the FTC will collect more than $1.1 million for consumer redress or disgorgement.

In *United States v. Luebke Baker*, the FTC obtained a settlement with a debt collector that allegedly sought to recover on bogus magazine subscription debts that it purchased from others.[39] The defendants repeatedly told consumers that these debts were valid even though the seller had provided the defendants with information indicating that some of them were not. The complaint also alleged that the defendants masked their identities over caller ID, falsely told consumers that magazine debts are exempt from statutes of limitations, and threatened to garnish wages and take other unintended legal actions. The settlement imposed a monetary judgment totaling $3.1 million, including $2.3 million in civil penalties for violations of the FDCPA and $730,000 in disgorgement for violations of the FTC Act. The judgments are suspended except for $20,000, based on the defendants' inability to pay.

The FTC also brought actions against companies that use false threats to collect on payday loans. In *FTC v. Goldman Schwartz,* the Southern District of Texas entered a temporary restraining order with asset freeze against a debt collector that the FTC alleged violated the FTC Act and the FDCPA by making false statements, including falsely threatening consumers with arrest; disclosing consumers' debts to third parties; collecting unauthorized fees; engaging in harassing and abusive conduct; failing to provide required notices; and making phone calls before 8:00 am and after 9:00 pm.[40] Similarly, in *FTC v. AMG Services, Inc.*, the FTC alleged that a payday lender, collecting on its own behalf, violated the FTC Act by falsely threatening to take legal action against consumers.[41] The parties have stipulated to a preliminary injunction that prohibits the payday lender from making misrepresentations while collecting debts.[42] The Commission continues to litigate the *Goldman Schwartz* and *AMG Services* cases.

5.2.2. Phantom Debt

The FTC reports that one of its major consumer protection concerns is the rise of entities that attempt to collect so-called "phantom debt," which is purported debt (often payday loans) that either does not exist, or for which the entity attempting to collect has no right to collect. Collectors of phantom debt engage in unfair, deceptive, or abusive conduct and portray themselves as legitimate debt collectors. In the past year, the FTC has filed or resolved three actions against this fraudulent activity.

On October 10, 2012, in *FTC v. American Credit Crunchers*, the federal court in the Northern District of Illinois entered a settlement agreement that includes a $5.4 million judgment as part of a permanent injunction against the defendants for violations of the FTC Act and the FDCPA.[43] The judgment was partially suspended based on inability to pay, although the defendants were required to turn over assets worth approximately $170,000. The complaint alleged that employees of the company pretended to be law enforcement or other government authorities, and falsely threatened to arrest and jail consumers immediately if they did not agree to make payment on purportedly delinquent payday loans.[44] The complaint charged that information consumers submitted in applying for payday loans online found its way into the defendants' hands. Even though consumers did not receive a payday loan from any lender that had retained the defendants to collect, defendants typically demanded more than $300, and sometimes as much as $2,000, from consumers.

Many consumers believed these demands were legitimate because the defendants had their Social Security or bank account numbers from their payday loan applications.

In *FTC v. Pro Credit Group, LLC*, the FTC charged that several of the defendants, working closely with overseas call centers, engaged in a scheme to defraud consumers by processing payments for debts, including payday loans that the consumers did not owe, or were never applied to the consumers' actual debts.[45] As in *American Credit Crunchers,* callers often claimed that they were law enforcement personnel and threatened consumers with arrest or other legal action. The United States District Court for the Middle District of Florida entered a preliminary injunction against the defendants and the litigation is ongoing.

Finally, in *FTC v. Broadway Global Master, Inc.*, the FTC charged the defendants with making more than 2.7 million phantom debt collection calls to at least 600,000 different phone numbers nationwide.[46] The FTC asserted that the defendants fraudulently collected more than $5.2 million in less than two years from consumers, many of whom were strapped for cash and thought the money they were paying would be applied to loans they owed. The court granted a preliminary injunction with an asset freeze. The litigation is ongoing. In August 2012, in a parallel criminal proceeding, a federal grand jury charged the owner of Broadway Global with 21 criminal counts of wire and mail fraud for his phantom debt collection scheme.[47]

5.2.3. Other Law Enforcement Activities

5.2.3.a. Private Plaintiffs' Rights: Marx Amicus brief

As explained in Section 5.1.2 above, in August 2012, the FTC joined the CFPB and the Department of Justice in filing an amicus brief in the Supreme Court urging the Court to rule that private plaintiffs who file good-faith lawsuits against debt collectors for alleged violations of the FDCPA are not required to pay prevailing defendants' litigation costs.[48] In the underlying case, a consumer, Olivea Marx, sued a debt collector that had contacted her employer to obtain information about her employment status. Marx believed that the debt collector's conduct had violated the FDCPA, but she lost the case. The United States Court of Appeals for the Tenth Circuit ruled that Marx was responsible for paying more than $4,500 to cover the debt collector's litigation costs, even though she had brought the case in good faith.

The federal government's amicus brief argued that the Tenth Circuit's decision was inconsistent with the FDCPA, which states that if a court finds that an FDCPA action "was brought in bad faith and for the purpose of harassment, [it] may award to the defendant attorney's fees reasonable in relation to the work expended and costs." The federal government also argued that limiting the imposition of litigation costs to consumers acting in bad faith or for harassment advances Congress' intent to deter unlawful debt collection practices through good faith private FDCPA actions. In contrast, the Tenth Circuit's ruling would create a disincentive to the prosecution of private enforcement actions.

The Supreme Court heard oral argument on the matter on November 7, 2012 and on February 26, 2013, issued a decision affirming the Tenth Circuit's ruling.

5.2.4. Time-Barred Debt: RJM Acquisitions Closing Letter

An ongoing issue in the debt collection industry is what debt collectors must tell consumers in connection with collecting on debt that is beyond the relevant statute of limitations, also known as time-barred debt.[49] In early 2012, the defendant agreed to settle *United States v. Asset Acceptance*, LLC, in which the FTC alleged that, in attempting to collect on debts that it knew or should have known were time-barred, Asset created the misleading impression that it could sue consumers if they did not pay.[50] The FTC alleged that Asset's failure to disclose to consumers that it could not legally sue consumers if they did not pay was a deceptive practice violating Section 5 of the FTC Act. To remedy the alleged violation, Asset agreed to a settlement requiring among other things that, for any debt that Asset knows or should know is time-barred, Asset disclose that it will not sue to collect on it.

In August 2012, the FTC's staff closed its investigation of RJM Acquisitions LLC ("RJM") for possible FDCPA violations concerning time-barred debt.[51] RJM is a debt buyer that attempts to collect on debts it purchases from original creditors, some of which are time-barred. The staff's closing letter explained that, even in the absence of any affirmative representations that consumers will be sued to collect time-barred debt, merely attempting to collect on such debt may lead consumers to believe that such suits may occur. Misleading consumers in this way would violate Section 5 of the FTC Act and Section 807 of the FDCPA. In its closing letter to RJM, FTC staff noted that RJM had added a disclosure to its collection letters to avoid consumers taking away the impression that they can be sued to collect on time-barred debt.

6. Education and Outreach Initiatives

6.1. Bureau Education and Outreach Initiatives

The Bureau's Consumer Education and Engagement ("CEE") division helps empower consumers to make financial decisions that work for themselves and their families through wide-ranging consumer education efforts. These efforts include targeted outreach to special consumer populations as required by the Dodd-Frank Act. These special populations include students, older Americans, servicemembers and veterans.

CEE creates an interactive, informative relationship between consumers and the Bureau to link consumers to information about specific financial decisions, including those relating to debt collection, and to help inform the Bureau's policymaking. One of CEE's initiatives is Ask CFPB, an interactive online tool that helps consumers find clear, unbiased, authoritative answers to their financial questions.

- As of January 2013, there were:
  - 918 consumer questions answered in Ask CFPB; and,
  - More than 187,000 unique visitors since launch in March 2012
- Topics include debt collection, and also credit cards, mortgages, bank accounts and services, student loans, auto loans, consumer loans, prepaid cards, and credit reports and scores.

Ask CFPB for debt collections was initiated on October 21, 2012. The Ask CFPB questions and answers on debt collection address a wide range of issues under the FDCPA, including the meaning of specific terms, consumers' rights, and debt collectors' authorities and obligations.[52] The questions and answers address many specific debt collection topics, including debt settlement, debt settlement services and credit counseling, as well as other federal and state laws that may apply to debt collection practices. Where appropriate, Ask CFPB provides practical tips to consumers regarding steps they can take to exercise their rights under the FDCPA or better manage delinquent debt.

Ask CFPB also includes FAQs targeted to special consumer populations. For example, one segment of the debt collection FAQs address issues related to the debt of someone who is deceased, which may be most relevant to older adults. There are also segments of the FAQs that address collection of student loan debts, as well as the rights, obligations, and specific circumstances of servicemembers and their families.

6.1.1. Student Lending

Delinquency and default often receive less attention in the larger debt collection discussion, but are a quickly growing segment of outstanding student loan debt. Over a quarter of all student loan borrowers are at least one monthly payment behind. Millions of federal student loan borrowers have defaulted on their loans. Both private and federal student loans cannot be discharged through bankruptcy absent a demonstration of "undue hardship," a very narrow exception that makes relief through bankruptcy inaccessible for most borrowers.

These borrowers, like many Americans, were hit hard by the recession. The unemployment rate among young college graduates is more than twice the rate of their older counterparts. Of those who have found work, more than a third of college graduates under age 25 have taken jobs that do not require a college degree. These young adults will feel the impact of graduating into a recession for a decade or more; it will take 10 to 15 years for their salaries to catch up to those who had the benefit of graduating into a healthy job market.

Over the past decade, student debt has grown by over 20% to average over $22,000 for graduates of public colleges and universities and over $28,000 for private school grads. A growing number of borrowers, greater than one in eight, have debts of $50,000 or more. For many, this economic reality makes producing each loan payment in full and on time a monthly struggle.

Last year, the Bureau released a web tool, Repay Student Debt, for borrowers who have fallen behind on their student loan payments. The tool has helped borrowers understand their options; communicate effectively with their loan servicer or debt collector; and work to bring their loans out of default or delinquency. Addressing the problems of delinquency and default provides these borrowers with opportunities to rebuild their credit, go back to school, or buy a home.

For borrowers with private student loans, options to cure a student loan in default may be limited. In February, the Bureau announced an effort to better understand ways to spur more affordable private student loan repayment options, including alternatives for borrowers that are delinquent or in default. The Bureau is soliciting ideas from borrowers and stakeholders in the private student lending marketplace and will share its findings with the public later this year.

6.2. FTC Education and Public Outreach

The second prong of the FTC's FDCPA program is education and public outreach. Consumer education informs consumers of their rights under the FDCPA and what the statute requires of debt collectors. Business education informs debt collectors what they must do to comply with the law. The FTC also engages in public outreach to enhance legal service providers' understanding of debt collection issues.

The FTC educates consumers through English and Spanish written materials, one-on-one guidance, and speeches and presentations. In 2012, the Commission supplemented its distribution of this information by launching two consumer-oriented websites: consumer.ftc.gov and consumer.gov. Launched in December 2012, Consumer.ftc.gov offers straightforward articles about a variety of consumer protection topics, as well as videos, educational games, and a blog that invites consumer comments.[53] The site addresses debt collection topics ranging from phantom debt collection[54] to time-barred debts.[55] Consumer.gov, which launched in October 2012, is the product of extensive work in coordination with the Center for Applied Linguistics to write and design the site for audiences with low literacy levels. Features include short videos, infographics, and read-along audio. The site includes basic material on a variety of consumer protection topics, including a section about dealing with debt collectors. Material on both sites is available in English and Spanish.

The FTC educates industry by developing and distributing business education materials, delivering speeches, participating in panel discussions at industry conferences, and providing interviews to general media and trade publications. A complete list of the FTC's consumer and business education materials relating to debt collection and information on the extent of their distribution is set forth in Appendix A.

Finally, as part of the FTC's Legal Services Collaboration project, FTC staff regularly meets with legal services providers to discuss various consumer protection issues, including the FTC's work in the debt collection arena. In March 2012, FTC staff provided information about the agency's debt collection work in a webinar hosted by the National Association for Consumer Advocates. In October 2012, the FTC hosted legal service providers and other government agencies at a Washington, DC conference that had a strong focus on debt collection issues. The FTC also organizes "Common Ground" conferences that bring together legal services providers and law enforcement to discuss a wide variety of consumer protection issues, including debt collection. In 2012, Common Ground conferences were held in Phoenix, Concord (NH), Chicago, San Francisco, and Seattle.

7. RESEARCH AND POLICY INITIATIVES

7.1. Bureau Research and Policy Initiatives

The Research, Markets, and Regulations ("RMR") division of the Bureau is responsible for analyzing consumer financial markets and consumer behavior, providing analytics to support the Offices of Fair Lending, Supervision and Enforcement, identifying areas where there is a need to consider improving the functions of a particular consumer financial market, developing and prioritizing policy initiatives in various market areas, identifying and analyzing alternative policy approaches, and, where a decision is made to proceed through regulation, developing the rules themselves.

The Deposits, Cash, Collections & Reporting Markets office is responsible for the debt collection and debt buying market. Throughout the year, RMR did considerable outreach to industry and stake holder groups. In regard to the collections industry, CFPB staff has spoken at association conferences (*Debt Buyers Association, The Association of Credit and Collections Professionals (ACA), The National Association of Retail Collection Attorneys*), vendor conferences (*Ontario Systems*), and conferences sponsored by industry press (*The National Collections and Credit Risk Conference, the Collections and Recovery Solutions Conference, and the Credit & Collections News Conference*). CFPB staff has also addressed the consumer credit counseling associations (*The Association of Independent Consumer Credit Counseling Agencies and The Association of Credit Counseling Professionals*).

The CFPB has also held meetings with many individual stakeholders, industry, consumer groups, vendors, and associations to better understand the debt collection industry and eco- system. Meetings have been held with many of the largest debt collectors, credit issuers, consumer advocacy groups, technologists, and state regulators to understand their issues and positions so that potential future regulatory intervention is well informed. Consumer groups CFPB met with include *Center for Responsible Lending* and *National Consumer Law Center*.

7.2. FTC Research and Policy Development Activities

The third prong of the FTC's FDCPA program is research and policy initiatives. In the past year, the FTC has continued to monitor and evaluate the debt collection industry and its practices. Specifically, as described below, the FTC has examined the role of debt buying and new technologies in the debt collection industry.

7.2.1. Debt Buyer Study

Debt buying has become a significant part of the debt collection system over the past decade, and many debts are purchased and resold several times over a period of years before collection efforts finally cease. To empirically evaluate information flow concerns and related issues, the FTC undertook a study of the debt buying industry. In December 2009, the FTC issued orders to nine of the nation's largest debt buying companies, requiring them to produce extensive and detailed information about their practices in buying and selling consumer debt.

On January 30, 2013, the FTC released its report on the debt buying industry. The report analyzed more than 5,000 portfolios of consumer debt containing nearly 90 million consumer accounts with a face value of $143 billion. The report explained that debt buyers typically receive certain information from creditors at the time of purchase, but seldom receive certain key information and documentation about the debt, such as the dispute history or outstanding balances broken down by principal, interest, and fees. As the report indicates, there is room for improvement in the information these companies have when they contact consumers and try to collect. As the FTC has noted previously,[56] the limited information that debt buyers receive may make it more likely that they will attempt to collect from the wrong consumer or the wrong amount.

The FTC study also estimated that consumers disputed 3.2% of the debts that debt buyers said they owed—at least one million disputed debts per year in the debt buyer industry. The FTC concluded that "the proper handling of this large number of disputed debts is a significant consumer protection concern." In addition, the study revealed that debt buyers verified only half of the debts consumers disputed, and they were less likely to verify debts if they were older. The report cites the need for further research into issues relating to debt buying.

7.2.2. Debt Collection 2.0 Workshop

In April 2011, the FTC convened industry representatives, consumer advocates, regulators, researchers and others to discuss debt collection technologies at a public workshop, *Debt Collection 2.0: Protecting Consumers as Technologies Change.*[57] Since the FDCPA was enacted in 1977, technologies for collecting and transmitting data, communicating, and making payments have advanced. Today's collectors, for example, increasingly communicate with consumers via electronic mail, mobile phones, text messaging, and social media. In connection with these developments, workshop participants discussed the following topics: how debt collection technologies have evolved in recent years; whether such technologies can increase the likelihood collectors will contact the right consumer seeking the right amount; how to weigh the costs and benefits to consumers and collectors of employing newer technologies for information collection and storage, communication, and payment; and whether any legal or policy reforms might enhance consumer protection.

The insights gained through the workshop have been and will continue to be valuable in the FTC's law enforcement investigations and litigation in the debt collection area. Further, over the past year, FTC staff has discussed its findings with CFPB staff working on debt collection issues. The Commission anticipates that these consultations will be instrumental in the CFPB's ongoing and future efforts to administer and enforce the FDCPA and other laws implicated by debt collection technologies.

8. Cooperation and Coordination between the Bureau and the FTC

As required by the Dodd-Frank Act, the Bureau and the FTC have and will continue to work together to coordinate their enforcement activities to promote consistent regulatory treatment of consumer financial products and services.

In January 2012, the Bureau and the FTC entered into a Memorandum of Understanding ("MOU") to coordinate efforts to protect consumers and avoid duplication of federal law enforcement and regulatory efforts.[58] In the MOU, the agencies have supplemented the requirements of the Dodd-Frank Act to create a strong and comprehensive framework for coordination and cooperation. Among other things the two agencies have agreed to:

- Meet regularly to coordinate upcoming law enforcement, rulemaking, and other activities.
- Inform the other agency, absent exigent circumstances, prior to initiating an investigation or bringing an enforcement action. This notice will prevent duplicative or conflicting enforcement efforts and undue burdens on industry.
- Consult on rulemaking and guidance initiatives to promote consistency and reflect the experience and expertise of both agencies.
- Cooperate on consumer education efforts to promote consistency of messages and maximum use of resources.
- Share consumer complaints.

The MOU enables the Bureau and the FTC to work together to ensure fair and vigorous implementation of the FDCPA.

Conclusion

The Bureau will continue to develop its debt collection program over the coming year, and will work actively to protect consumers from the unfair, deceptive, and abusive conduct of some debt collectors. The Bureau looks forward to performing this work in cooperation with the FTC.[59]

APPENDIX A

United States of America
Federal Trade Commission
Washington, D.C. 20580

February 1, 2013

The Honorable Richard Cordray
Director
Consumer Financial Protection Bureau
1801 L Street NW
Washington, DC 20036

Dear Mr. Cordray:

Thank you for your letter of December 11, 2012. As your letter mentions, the Consumer Financial Protection Bureau (CFPB) is responsible for providing annual reports to Congress concerning the federal government's efforts to implement the Fair Debt Collection Practices Act (FDCPA).[60] This letter describes the efforts the Federal Trade Commission (Commission or FTC) has taken during the past year in the debt collection arena. In the FTC's debt collection work, the CFPB has been a valuable partner, and the Commission anticipates that our partnership will become even stronger in the future. We hope that the information in this letter will assist the CFPB in preparing this year's report.

I. The Commission's Debt Collection Program

The FTC's debt collection program is a three-pronged effort: (1) vigorous law enforcement; (2) education and public outreach; and (3) research and policy initiatives. Over the past year, the FTC has employed all three prongs in its effort to curtail illegal debt collection practices and protect consumers.

As described in detail below, last year, the Commission continued to engage in aggressive law enforcement activities to address troubling debt collection activity and obtained strong remedies to promote compliance with the law. The FTC educated consumers about their rights and businesses about their responsibilities under the FDCPA and the FTC Act. The FTC also consulted regularly with the public as part of the agency's debt collection outreach efforts. And the Commission engaged in research and policy development activities to identify, adopt, and advocate debt collection policies and practices that advance the agency's consumer protection mission.

II. Law Enforcement Activities

The Commission is primarily a law enforcement agency, and law enforcement investigations and litigation are at the heart of the FTC's recent debt collection work. Both the FDCPA and the FTC Act authorize the Commission to investigate and take law enforcement action against debt collectors that violate those statutes.[61] If an FTC investigation reveals that a debt collector violated the law, the Commission may file a federal court action seeking injunctive relief under Section 13(b) of the FTC Act or refer the matter to the Department of Justice. Where a collector's violations are so egregious that a court order is necessary to halt the conduct immediately, or where consumer redress and disgorgement are more appropriate forms of monetary relief than civil penalties, the FTC generally files the action itself under Section 13(b) of the FTC Act. Where, on the other hand, preliminary injunctive relief to halt unlawful conduct is unnecessary and civil penalties are appropriate monetary relief, the FTC may refer the case to the Department of Justice.

In addition to filing and referring law enforcement actions, the FTC files amicus briefs and undertakes other law enforcement related activities.

A. Legal Actions

In recent years, to improve deterrence, the Commission has focused on bringing a greater number of cases and obtaining stronger monetary and injunctive remedies against debt collectors that violate the law. Over the past year, the FTC has brought or resolved seven debt collection cases, matching the highest number of debt collection cases that it has brought or resolved in any single year. In each of its six Section 13(b) cases[62] involving debt collection, the FTC obtained preliminary or permanent injunctive relief. In many of these cases, the preliminary relief that was obtained included ex parte temporary restraining orders with asset freezes, immediate access to business premises, and appointment of receivers to run the debt collection business.

The cases discussed below represent a concerted effort by the FTC to target inappropriate debt collection practices including false threats, harassment or abuse, and attempts to collect on phantom payday loan debts.

1. Deceptive, Unfair, and Abusive Collector Conduct

Targeting debt collectors that engage in deceptive, unfair, or abusive conduct continues to be one of the Commission's highest priorities. In the past year, the Commission has filed or resolved four such actions. In *FTC v. Forensic Case Management Services, Inc.*, after over a year of litigation, the FTC has secured substantial monetary judgments against a debt collection enterprise and a complete ban on future debt collection activity, along with other injunctive relief.[63] The FTC's complaint alleged that the defendants violated the FTC Act and the FDCPA through such egregious conduct as threatening to physically harm consumers and desecrate the bodies of their dead relatives; threatening to kill consumers' pets; using obscene and profane language; revealing consumers' debts to third parties; and falsely threatening consumers with lawsuits, arrest, and wage garnishment. The FTC entered into settlements with six individuals and three corporations responsible for the enterprise, as well as three relief defendants, for judgments totaling over $35.5 million.[64] The judgments were partially suspended based on the defendants' inability to pay, although the FTC will collect more than $1.1 million for consumer redress or disgorgement.

In *United States v. Luebke Baker*, the Commission obtained a settlement with a debt collector that allegedly sought to recover on bogus magazine subscription debts that it purchased from others.[65] The defendants repeatedly told consumers that these debts were valid even though the seller had provided the defendants with information indicating that some of them were not. The complaint also alleged that the defendants masked their identities over caller ID, falsely told consumers that magazine debts are exempt from statutes of limitations, and threatened to garnish wages and take other unintended legal actions. The settlement imposed a monetary judgment totaling $3.1 million, including $2.3 million in civil penalties for violations of the FDCPA and $730,000 in disgorgement for violations of the FTC Act. The judgments are suspended except for $20,000, based on the defendants' inability to pay.

The FTC also brought actions against companies that use false threats to collect on payday loans. In *FTC v. Goldman Schwartz*, the Southern District of Texas entered a temporary restraining order with asset freeze against a debt collector that the FTC alleged violated the FTC Act and the FDCPA by making false statements, including falsely threatening consumers with arrest; disclosing consumers' debts to third parties; collecting unauthorized fees; engaging in harassing and abusive conduct; failing to provide required notices; and making phone calls before 8:00am and after 9:00 pm.[66] Similarly, in *FTC v. AMG Services, Inc.*, the FTC alleged that a payday lender, collecting on its own behalf, violated the FTC Act by falsely threatening to take legal action against consumers.[67] The parties have stipulated to a preliminary injunction that prohibits the payday lender from making misrepresentations while collecting debts.[68] The Commission continues to litigate the *Goldman Schwartz* and *AMG Services* cases.

2. Phantom Debt Collection

One of the Commission's major consumer protection concerns is the rise of so-called "phantom debt collectors." Phantom debt collectors engage in unfair, deceptive, or abusive conduct by attempting to collect on debts (often related to payday loans) that either do not exist or are not owed to the phantom debt collector. In the past year, the Commission has filed or resolved three actions against phantom debt collectors.

On October 10, 2012, in *FTC v. American Credit Crunchers*, the federal court in the Northern District of Illinois entered a settlement agreement that includes a $5.4 million judgment as part of a permanent injunction against the defendants for violations of the FTC Act and the FDCPA.[69] The judgment was partially suspended based on inability to pay, although the defendants were required to turn over assets worth approximately $170,000. The complaint alleged that employees of the company pretended to be law enforcement or other government authorities, and falsely threatened to arrest and jail consumers immediately if they did not agree to make payment on purportedly delinquent payday loans.[70] The complaint charged that information consumers submitted in applying for payday loans online found its way into the defendants' hands. Even though consumers did not receive a payday loan from any lender that had retained the defendants to collect, defendants typically demanded more than $300, and sometimes as much as $2,000, from consumers. Many consumers believed these demands were legitimate because the defendants had their Social Security or bank account numbers from their payday loan applications.

In *FTC v. Pro Credit Group, LLC*, the FTC charged that several of the defendants, working closely with overseas call centers, engaged in a scheme to defraud consumers by processing payments for debts, including payday loans, that the consumers did not owe, or were never applied to the consumers' actual debts.[71] As in *American Credit Crunchers*, callers often claimed that they were law enforcement personnel and threatened consumers with arrest or other legal action. The United States District Court for the Middle District of Florida entered a preliminary injunction against the defendants and the litigation is ongoing.

Finally, in *FTC v. Broadway Global Master, Inc.*, the FTC charged the defendants with making more than 2.7 million phantom debt collection calls to at least 600,000 different phone numbers nationwide.[72] The FTC asserted that the defendants fraudulently collected more than $5.2 million in less than two years from consumers, many of whom were strapped for cash and thought the money they were paying would be applied to loans they owed. The court granted a preliminary injunction with an asset freeze. The litigation is ongoing. In August 2012, in a parallel criminal proceeding, a federal grand jury charged the owner of Broadway Global with 21 criminal counts of wire and mail fraud for his phantom debt collection scheme.[73]

B. Other Law Enforcement Activities

1. Private Plaintiffs' Rights: *Marx* Amicus Brief

In August 2012, the Commission joined the CFPB and the Department of Justice in filing an amicus brief in the Supreme Court urging the Court to rule that private plaintiffs who file good-faith lawsuits against debt collectors for alleged violations of the FDCPA are not required to pay prevailing defendants' litigation costs.[74] In the underlying case, a consumer, Olivea Marx, sued a debt collector that had contacted her employer to obtain information about her employment status. Marx believed that the debt collector's conduct had violated the FDCPA, but she lost the case. The United States Court of Appeals for the Tenth Circuit ruled that Marx was responsible for paying more than $4,500 to cover the debt collector's litigation costs, even though she had brought the case in good faith.

The federal government's amicus brief argues that the Tenth Circuit's decision was inconsistent with the FDCPA, which states that if a court finds that an FDCPA action "was brought in bad faith and for the purpose of harassment, [it] may award to the defendant attorney's fees reasonable in relation to the work expended and costs." The federal government also argues that limiting the imposition of litigation costs to consumers acting in bad faith or for harassment advances Congress' intent to deter unlawful debt collection practices through good faith private FDCPA actions. In contrast, the Tenth Circuit's ruling would create a disincentive to the prosecution of private enforcement actions.

The Supreme Court heard oral argument on the matter on November 7, 2012.

2. Time-Barred Debt: RJM Acquisitions Closing Letter

An ongoing issue in the debt collection industry is what debt collectors must tell consumers in connection with collecting on debt that are beyond the relevant statute of limitations, also known as time-barred debt.[75] In 2011, the defendant agreed to settle *United States v. Asset Acceptance, LLC*, in which the Commission alleged that, in attempting to collect on debts that it knew or should have known were time-barred, Asset created the misleading impression that it could sue consumers if they did not pay.[76] The Commission alleged that Asset's failure to disclose to consumers that it could not legally sue consumers if they did not pay was a deceptive practice violating Section 5 of the FTC Act. To remedy the alleged violation, Asset agreed to a settlement requiring among other things that, for any debt that Asset knows or should know is time-barred, Asset disclose that it will not sue to collect on it.

In August 2012, the Commission's staff closed its investigation of RJM Acquisitions LLC ("RJM") for possible FDCPA violations concerning time-barred debt.[77] RJM is a debt buyer that attempts to collect on debts it purchases from original creditors, some of which are time-barred. The staff's closing letter explained that, even in the absence of any affirmative representations that consumers will be sued to collect time-barred debt, merely attempting to collect on such debt may lead consumers to believe that such suits may occur. Misleading consumers in this way would violate Section 5 of the FTC Act and Section 807 of the FDCPA. In its closing letter to RJM, FTC staff noted that RJM had added a disclosure to its collection letters to avoid consumers taking away the impression that they can be sued to collect on time-barred debt.

III. Education and Public Outreach

The second prong of the FTC's FDCPA program is education and public outreach. Consumer education informs consumers of their rights under the FDCPA and what the statute requires of debt collectors. Business education informs debt collectors what they must do to comply with the law. The FTC also engages in public outreach to enhance legal service providers' understanding of debt collection issues.

The Commission educates consumers through English and Spanish written materials, one- on-one guidance, and speeches and presentations. In 2012, the Commission supplemented its distribution of this information by launching two consumer-oriented websites: consumer.ftc.gov and consumer.gov. Consumer.ftc.gov, which launched in December 2012, offers straightforward articles about a variety of consumer protection topics, as well as videos, educational games, and a blog that invites consumer comments.[78] The site addresses debt collection topics ranging from phantom debt collection[79] to time-barred debts.[80] Consumer.gov, which launched in October 2012, is the product of extensive work in coordination with the Center for Applied Linguistics to write and design the site for audiences with low literacy levels. Features include short videos, infographics, and read-along audio. The site includes basic material on a variety of consumer protection topics, including a section about dealing with debt collectors. Material on both sites is available in English and Spanish.

The Commission educates industry by developing and distributing business education materials, delivering speeches, participating in panel discussions at industry conferences, and providing interviews to general media and trade publications. A complete list of the FTC's consumer and business education materials relating to debt collection and information on the extent of their distribution is set forth in Appendix A to this letter.

Finally, as part of the FTC's Legal Services Collaboration project, FTC staff regularly meets with legal services providers to discuss various consumer protection issues, including the FTC's work in the debt collection arena. In March 2012, FTC staff provided information about the agency's debt collection work in a webinar hosted by the National Association for Consumer Advocates. In October 2012, the FTC hosted legal service providers and other government agencies at a Washington, DC conference that had a strong focus on debt collection issues. The FTC also organizes "Common Ground" conferences that bring together legal services providers and law enforcement to discuss a wide variety of consumer protection issues, including debt collection. In 2012, Common Ground conferences were held in Phoenix, Concord (NH), Chicago, San Francisco, and Seattle.

IV. Research and Policy Development Activities

The third prong of the FTC's FDCPA program is research and policy initiatives. In the past year, the FTC has continued to monitor and evaluate the debt collection industry and its practices. Specifically, as described below, the FTC has examined the role of debt buying and new technologies in the debt collection industry.

A. Debt Buyer Study

Debt buying has become a significant part of the debt collection system over the past decade, and many debts are purchased and resold several times over a period of years before collection efforts finally cease. Some commentators have suggested that the age, amount, and quality of debt-related information that is sold results in debt collectors increasingly seeking to collect from the wrong consumer, in the wrong amount, or both. To empirically evaluate these information flow concerns and related issues, the Commission undertook a study of the debt buying industry. In December 2009, the FTC issued orders to nine of the nation's largest debt buying companies, requiring them to produce extensive and detailed information about their practices in buying and selling consumer debt.

On January 30, 2013, the FTC released its report on the debt buying industry. The report analyzed more than 5,000 portfolios of consumer debt containing nearly 90 million consumer accounts with a face value of $143 billion. The report explained that debt buyers typically receive certain information from creditors at the time of purchase, but seldom receive certain key information and documentation about the debt, such as the dispute history or outstanding balances broken down by principal, interest, and fees. As the report indicates, there is room for improvement in the information these companies have when they contact consumers and try to collect. As the Commission has noted previously,[81] the limited information that debt buyers receive may make it more likely that they will attempt to collect from the wrong consumer or the wrong amount.

The FTC study also estimated that consumers disputed 3.2% of the debts that debt buyers said they owed—at least one million disputed debts per year in the debt buyer industry. The Commission concluded that "the proper handling of this large number of disputed debts is a significant consumer protection concern." In addition, the study revealed that debt buyers verified only half of the debts consumers disputed, and they were less likely to verify debts if they were older. The report cites the need for further research into issues relating to debt buying.

B. Debt Collection 2.0 Workshop

In April 2011, the FTC convened industry representatives, consumer advocates, regulators, researchers and others to discuss debt collection technologies at a public workshop, *Debt Collection 2.0: Protecting Consumers as Technologies Change.*[82] Since the FDCPA was enacted in 1977, technologies for collecting and transmitting data, communicating, and making payments have advanced. Today's collectors, for example, increasingly communicate with consumers via electronic mail, mobile phones, text messaging, and social media. In connection with these developments, workshop participants discussed the following topics: how debt collection technologies have evolved in recent years; whether such technologies can increase the likelihood collectors will contact the right consumer seeking the right amount; how to weigh the costs and benefits to consumers and collectors of employing newer technologies for information collection and storage, communication, and payment; and whether any legal or policy reforms might enhance consumer protection.

The insights gained through the workshop have been and will continue to be valuable in the FTC's law enforcement investigations and litigation in the debt collection area. Further, over the past year, FTC staff has discussed its findings with CFPB staff working on debt collection issues. The Commission anticipates that these consultations will be instrumental in the CFPB's ongoing and future efforts to administer and enforce the FDCPA and other laws implicated by debt collection technologies.

V. Conclusion

The Commission hopes that the information contained in this letter will assist the CFPB in its annual report to Congress about its administration of the FDCPA. The FTC looks forward to continuing to cooperate and coordinate with the CFPB on consumer protection issues relating to debt collection. If any other information would be useful or if you wish to request additional assistance, please contact Jessica Rich, Associate Director, Division of Financial Practices, at (202) 326-3224.

By direction of the Commission,
Donald S. Clark
Secretary

Debt Collection Educational Material Distribution in 2012[83]

Consumer or Business Educational Material	Offline Distribution		Online Access	
	English	Spanish	English	Spanish
Consumer Education: Brochures				
Credit and Your Consumer Rights	58,100	7,200	35,741	3,221
Settling Your Credit Card Debts	44,200	6,900	2,689	2,954
Debt Collection FAQs: A Guide for Consumers	35,300	6,300	469,831	6,356
Knee-Deep in Debt	48,300	6,400	186,183	5,960
Debt Collection Arbitration: The Who, What, Why and How	25,800	N/A	13,245	N/A
Consumer Education: Alerts (Online Only)				
Paying the Debts of a Deceased Relative: Who is Responsible?	N/A	N/A	13,464	1,513
Ads Offering Debt Relief	N/A	N/A	3,845	1,026
Creditors Seeking Federal Benefits in Your Bank Account? Understanding Your Rights	N/A	N/A	14,525	N/A
Time-Barred Debts	N/A	N/A	79,650	3,003
Who's Calling? That Debt Collector Could Be a Fake	N/A	N/A	29,259	1,351
Consumer Education: Video (Online Only)				
Debt Collection, Animated	N/A	N/A	30,180	4,294
Business Education: Brochures				
The Fair Debt Collection Practices Act	N/A	N/A	310,127	N/A
Business Education: Video (Online Only)				
Debt Collection	N/A	N/A	4,588	N/A

APPENDIX B

Year	2012	2011
Total Debt Collection ("DC") Complaints	125,136	144,451
DC Complaints as Percentage of All FTC Complaints[84]	24.1%	27.5%
Total Third-Party DC Complaints	102,783	118,945
Third-Party DC Complaints as Percentage of All FTC Complaints	19.8%	22.6%
Total In-House DC Complaints	22,353	25,506
In-House DC Complaints as Percentage of All FTC Complaints	4.3%	4.9%

APPENDIX C

FDCPA Complaint Category	Total 2012 Complaints	Percentage of 2012 FDCPA Complaints	2012 Category Rank	Total 2011 Complaints	Percentage of 2011 FDCPA Complaints	2011 Category Rank
Misrepresent Debt Character, Amount, or Status	39,993	38.9%	1	47,012	39.5%	2
Repeated Calls	37,543	36.5%	2	47,573	40.0%	1
Falsely Threatens Illegal or Unintended Act	30,470	29.6%	3	35,738	30.0%	3
No Written Notice	26,139	25.4%	4	30,753	25.9%	4
Falsely Threatens Arrest, Property Seizure	24,062	23.4%	5	27,270	22.9%	5
Fails to Identify as Debt Collector	17,873	17.4%	6	20,793	17.5%	6
Repeated Calls to Third Parties	16,679	16.2%	7	20,798	17.5%	7
Improperly Calls Debtor At Work	14,482	14.1%	8	16,932	14.2%	8
Uses Obscene, Profane, or Abusive Language	13,329	13.0%	9	16,610	14.0%	9
Reveals Debt to Third Party	12,272	11.9%	10	12,654	10.6%	10
Refuses to Verify Debt After Written Request	9,814	9.5%	11	10,002	8.4%	12
Collects Unauthorized Fees, Interest, or Expenses	9,034	8.8%	12	9,325	7.8%	13
Calls Before 8:00 a.m., after 9:00 p.m., or at Inconvenient Times	8,166	7.9%	13	10,494	8.8%	11
Calls Debtor After Getting "Cease Communication" Notice	4,928	4.8%	14	5,933	5.0%	14
Uses or Threatens Violence	3,312	3.2%	15	3,980	3.3%	15

End Notes

[1] Dodd-Frank Wall Street Reform and Consumer Protection Act ("Dodd-Frank Act"), Pub. L. No. 111-203, § 1089, 124 Stat. 1376, 2092-93 (2010) (amending the FDCPA, 15 U.S.C. § 1692 *et seq.*).

[2] *See*, e.g., Dodd-Frank Act §§ 1013, 1021, 1061, 1089 (2010).

[3] *See* 15 U.S.C. § 1692m(b) (providing that the Bureau may obtain for the annual report the views of any other federal agency which exercises enforcement functions under the FDCPA).

[4] Federal Reserve Bank of New York, Quarterly Report on Household Debt and Credit (November 2012), *available at* http://www.newyorkfed.org/research/national_economy/householdcredit/DistrictReport_Q32012.pdf.

[5] 15 U.S.C. § 1692(a).

[6] Id.

[7] *See* Dodd-Frank Act, Pub. L. No. 111-203, § 1021(c)(2), (2010).

[8] Consumers may file complaints with the FTC via its toll-free hotline (1-877-FTC-HELP), online complaint forms at https://www.ftccomplaintassistant.gov, or United States mail.

[9] The 2011 complaint numbers identified in this year's report differ slightly from those identified in last year's report because, in connection with a quality assurance review, the FTC staff reviewed and re-coded some complaints after the 2012 Annual Report was issued.

[10] In general, consumer complaints concern the alleged behavior of specific actors, whereas consumer inquiries ask for information about their legal rights or other topics.

[11] In contrast, the Federal Trade Commission's Annual Consumer Sentinel Network Data Book includes in the complaint numbers the complaints submitted to certain other entities that partner with the FTC in Consumer Sentinel, the agency's law enforcement complaint-sharing system. *See* FTC Consumer Sentinel Network Data Book: January-December 2012 (Feb. 2013) at 2-3 and 6, *available at* http://www.ftc.gov/sentinel/reports/sentinel-annual-reports/sentinel-cy2012.pdf. For this reason, the total number of debt collection complaints set forth in this report is less than the number stated in the FTC's Annual Consumer Sentinel Network Data Book.

[12] The FTC does not count in the total number of debt collection complaints any identity theft or Do Not Call Registry complaints that may involve debt collection. The FTC does not consider identity theft and Do Not Call complaints to be reports about any specific industry. Identity theft complaints are excluded because such complaints relate to a variety of actors, rather than a single industry. Do Not Call Registry complaints similarly are excluded because the complaints capture the actions of a variety of industries that use telemarketing to contact consumers. Note, however, that some identity theft and Do Not Call Registry complaints may implicate deceptive, unfair, or abusive debt collection practices. For example, a consumer may complain about suspected identity theft when a debt collector is contacting him or her about a debt he or she never incurred. To that extent, the FDCPA complaint data in this report may under-report consumer complaints about debt collection practices.

[13] The total number of debt collection complaints from all entities was 199,721 in 2012, up from 185,630 in 2011. *See* FTC Consumer Sentinel Network Data Book: January-December 2012 (Feb. 2013) at 6 and 81, *available at* http://www.ftc.gov/sentinel/reports/sentinel-annual-reports/sentinel-cy2012.pdf.

[14] "Third-party debt collectors" include contingency fee collectors and attorneys who regularly collect or attempt to collect, directly or indirectly, debts asserted to be owed or due another, as well as debt buyers collecting on debts they purchased in default.

[15] Some complaints are directed toward both third-party debt collectors and in-house creditor collectors. Thus, the total number of complaints against all debt collectors is slightly less than the sum of all third-party complaints and all in-house creditor complaints.

[16] *See* Appendix B for a chart showing the number of third-party collector complaints, in-house collector complaints, and total debt collector complaints in 2012 and 2011.

[17] Each CRC code assigned to an FDCPA complaint corresponds to a potential law violation.

[18] *See* Appendix C for a chart showing the number and percentage of FTC complaints for each FDCPA violation code in 2012 and 2011.

[19] 15 U.S.C. § 1692d.

[20] 15 U.S.C. §1692e(2).

[21] 15 U.S.C. § 1692f(1).

[22] 15 U.S.C. § 1692g(a).

[23] 15 U.S.C. § 1692e(4)-(5).

[24] 15 U.S.C. § 1692e(11). This requirement does not apply if the communication at issue is a formal pleading made in connection with a legal action. *Id.* 15 U.S.C. § 1692d(6) also provides that it is generally an abusive practice to place telephone calls without meaningful disclosure of the caller's identity.

[25] 15 U.S.C. § 1692c(b). Location information includes a consumer's home address and telephone number or place of employment. 15 U.S.C. § 1692a(7).

[26] 15 U.S.C. § 1692b(2).

[27] 15 U.S.C. § 1692b(3) prohibits a debt collector contacting a third party for location information from communicating with the third party more than once, unless the third party requests it or the collector reasonably believes the third party's earlier response was erroneous or incomplete and that the third party now has correct or complete location information.

[28] 15 U.S.C. § 1692c(a)(3).

[29] 15 U.S.C. § 1692g(b).

[30] 15 U.S.C. § 1692c(c).

[31] *See* Dodd-Frank Act § 1024(a)-(b)(2010); Dodd-Frank Act § 1024(e)(2010) (subjecting service providers to the Bureau's supervision authority, to the same extent that an appropriate Federal banking regulator would be able to supervise the service provider if it were in a service relationship with a bank, and requiring coordination with the appropriate prudential regulator, if applicable).

[32] 77 Fed.Reg. 65775 (October 31, 2012).

[33] Debt Collection Examination Procedures (Oct. 24, 2012), *available at* http://files.consumerfinance.gov/f/201210_cfpb_debt-collection-examination-procedures.pdf.

[34] *See* 12 C.F.R. pt. 1070; CFPB Bulletin 12-01 (Jan. 4, 2012), *available at* http://files.consumerfinance.gov/f/2012/01/GC_bulletin_12-01.pdf.

[35] *Birster v. Am. Home Mortg. Servicing, Inc.,* 481 Fed.Appx. 579 (11th Cir. 2012) (unpublished).

[36] Section 13(b) of the FTC Act, 15 U.S.C. § 53(b), authorizes the FTC to seek preliminary and permanent relief to remedy "any provision of law enforced by the Federal Trade Commission."

[37] Press Release, FTC Settlement Obtains Permanent Ban Against Abusive Debt Collection Operation (Jan. 17, 2013), *available at* http://www.ftc.gov/opa/2013/01/rumson.shtm.

[38] The Commission has moved for a default judgment against one minor relief defendant.

[39] *United States v. Luebke Baker & Associates, Inc.*, No. 1:12-cv-1145 (C.D. Ill. May 22, 2012) (stipulated final judgment and order); *see also* Press Release, Debt Collectors Settle with FTC, Agree to Stop Deceiving and Abusing Consumers (May 15, 2012), *available at* http://www.ftc.gov/opa/2012/05/luebkenr.shtm.

[40] Complaint, *FTC v. Goldman Schwartz,* No. 4:13-cv-106 (S.D. Tex. Jan. 31, 2013); *see also* Press Release, FTC Action Leads to Shutdown of Texas-based Debt Collector that Allegedly Used Deception, Insults, and False Threats Against Consumers (Jan. 31, 2013), *available at* http://www.ftc.gov/opa/2013/01/goldman.shtm.

[41] *Complaint, FTC v. AMG Services, Inc.*, No. 2:12-cv-536 (D. Nev. Apr. 2, 2012); *see also* Press Release, FTC Charges Payday Lending Scheme with Piling Inflated Fees on Borrowers and Making Unlawful Threats When Collecting (Apr. 2, 2012), *available at* http://www.ftc.gov/opa/2012/04/amg.shtm.

[42] *FTC v. AMG Services, Inc.*, No. 2:12-cv-536 (D. Nev. Dec. 27, 2012) (Order Entering Stipulated Preliminary Injunction and Bifurcation).

[43] *FTC v. American Credit Crunchers*, No. 12-CV-1028 (N.D. Ill. Oct. 10, 2012) (Stipulated Final Judgment and Order For Permanent Injunction); *see also* Press Release, U.S. Defendants Who Allegedly Abetted Fake Debt Collector Calls from India Agree to Settle FTC Charges (Oct. 23, 2012), *available at* http://www.ftc.gov/opa/2012/10/americancredit.shtm.

[44] *Complaint, FTC v. American Credit Crunchers*, No. 12-CV-1028 (N.D. Ill. Feb. 13, 2012); *see also* Press Release, Court Halts Alleged Fake Debt Collector Calls from India, Grants FTC Request to Stop Defendants Who Often Posed as Law Enforcement (Feb. 21, 2012), *available at* http://www.ftc.gov/opa/2012/02/acc.shtm.

[45] *Complaint, FTC v. Pro Credit Group, LLC, et al.,* No. 12-CV-586 (M.D. Fla. Mar. 19, 2012).

[46] Complaint, *FTC v. Broadway Global Master, Inc.*, No. 2:12-cv-855 (E.D. Cal. Apr. 3, 2012); *see also* Press Release, Court Halts Fake Debt Collector Calls from India, Grants FTC Request to Stop Defendants Who Posed as Law Enforcers (Apr. 11, 2012), *available at* http://www.ftc.gov/opa/2012/04/broadway.shtm.

[47] *U.S. Dep't of Justice, Press Release, Tracy Man Indicted for Phony Debt Collection Scam (Aug. 23, 2012), available at* http://www.justice.gov/usao/cae/news/docs/2012/08-2012/08-23-12Patel.html.

[48] *See* http://www.ftc.gov/opa/2012/08/amicus.shtm.

[49] See FTC, Repairing a Broken System: Protecting Consumers in Debt Collection Litigation and Arbitration at 25-28 (July 2010), *available at* http://www.ftc.gov/os/2010/07/debtcollectionreport.pdf.

[50] *United States v. Asset Acceptance, LLC, No. 8:12-cv-182-T-27EAJ (M.D. Fla. Jan. 31, 2012) (court entered order); see also* Press Release, Under FTC Settlement, Debt Buyer Agrees to Pay $2.5 Million for Alleged Consumer Deception (Jan. 30, 2012), *available at* http://www.ftc.gov/opa/2012/01/asset.shtm.

[51] *See* http://www.ftc.gov/os/closings/staff/120827rjmclosingletter.pdf.

[52] Consumers may find Ask CFPB debt collection questions and answers at http://www.consumerfinance.gov/askcfpb/search?selected_facets=category_exact:Debt Collection.

[53] *Welcome to the FTC's Home for Consumer Information* (Dec. 2012), *available at* www.consumer.ftc.gov/blog/welcome-ftcs-home-consumer-information.

[54] FTC, *Fake Debt Collectors* (Feb. 2012), *available at* www.consumer.ftc.gov/articles/0258-fake-debt-collectors.

[55] *FTC, Time-Barred Debts* (Jan. 2012), *available at* www.consumer.ftc.gov/articles/0117-time-barred-debts.

[56] Federal Trade Commission Annual Report 2010: Fair Debt Collection Practices Act at 17, available at http://www.ftc.gov/os/2010/04/P104802fdcpa2010annrpt.pdf; FTC, Collecting Consumer Debts: The Challenges of Change at iv-v; 21-24 (Feb. 2009), *available at* http://www.ftc.gov/bcp/workshops/debtcollection/dcwr.pdf.

[57] The final transcript of the workshop is available at www.ftc.gov/bcp/workshops/debtcollectiontech/docs/transcript.pdf.

[58] Memorandum of Understanding Between the Consumer Financial Protection Bureau and the Federal Trade Commission (Jan. 2012), *available at* http://ftc.gov/os/2012/01/120123ftc-cfpb-mou.pdf

[59] The Bureau would like to thank the FTC, and particularly David Torok and Reilly Dolan, for their valuable contributions to this report.

[60] The Dodd-Frank Act directed the CFPB to report to Congress on the federal government's implementation and administration of the FDCPA. Dodd-Frank Wall Street Reform and Consumer Protection Act (Dodd-Frank Act), Pub. L. 11-203, § 1089, 124 Stat. 1376, 2092-93 (2010) (amending the Fair Debt Collection Practices Act, 15 U.S.C. §§ 1692- 1692p). Prior to the enactment of the Dodd-Frank Act, Section 815(a) of the FDCPA, 15 U.S.C. § 1692m, required the FTC to report directly to Congress on these topics. The Commission submitted such annual reports from 1977 to 2011.

[61] The FDCPA authorizes the Commission to investigate and take law enforcement action against debt collectors that engage in unfair, deceptive, abusive, or other practices that violate the statute. Section 814 of the FDCPA, 15 U.S.C. § 1692l. Under the FTC Act, the FTC may investigate and take law enforcement action against entities that, in connection with collecting on debts, engage in unfair or deceptive acts and practices. Section 5 of the FTC Act, 15 U.S:C. § 45.

[62] The seventh case was a referral to the Department of Justice for civil penalties.

[63] Press Release, FTC Settlement Obtains Permanent Ban Against Abusive Debt Collection Operation (Jan. 17, 2013), *available at* http://www.ftc.gov/opa/2013/01/rumson.shtm.

[64] The Commission has moved for a default judgment against one minor relief defendant.

[65] *United States v. Luebke Baker & Associates, Inc.*, No. 1:12-cv-1145 (C.D. Ill. May 22, 2012) (stipulated final judgment and order); *see also* Press Release, Debt Collectors Settle with FTC, Agree to Stop Deceiving and Abusing Consumers (May 15, 2012), *available at* http://www.ftc.gov/opa/2012/05/luebkenr.shtm.

[66] Complaint, *FTC v. Goldman Schwartz*, No. 4:13-cv-00106 (S.D. Tex. Jan. 31, 2013); *see also* Press Release, FTC Action Leads to Shutdown of Texas-based Debt Collector that Allegedly Used Deception, Insults, and False Threats Against Consumers (Jan. 31, 2013), *available at* http://www.ftc.gov/opa/2013/01/goldman.shtm.

[67] *Complaint, FTC v. AMG Services, Inc.*, No. 2:12-cv-536 (D. Nev. Apr. 2, 2012); *see also* Press Release, FTC Charges Payday Lending Scheme with Piling Inflated Fees on Borrowers and Making Unlawful Threats While Collecting (Apr. 2, 2012), *available at* http://www.ftc.gov/opa/2012/04/amg.shtm.

[68] *FTC v. AMG Services, Inc.*, No. 2:12-cv-536 (D. Nev. Dec. 27, 2012) (Order Entering Stipulated Preliminary Injunction and Bifurcation).

[69] *FTC v. American Credit Crunchers*, No. 12-CV-1028 (N.D. Ill. Oct. 10, 2012) (Stipulated Final Judgment and Order For Permanent Injunction); *see also* Press Release, U.S. Defendants Who Allegedly Abetted Fake Debt Collector Calls from India Agree to Settle FTC Charges (Oct. 23, 2012), *available at* http://www.ftc.gov/opa/2012/10/americancredit.shtm.

[70] Complaint, *FTC v. American Credit Crunchers*, No. 12-CV-1028 (N.D. Ill. Feb. 13, 2012); *see also* Press Release, Court Halts Alleged Fake Debt Collector Calls from India, Grants FTC Request to Stop Defendants Who Often Posed as Law Enforcement (Feb. 21, 2012), *available at* http://www.ftc.gov/opa/2012/02/acc.shtm.

[71] *Complaint, FTC v. Pro Credit Group, LLC, et al.*, No. 12-CV-00586 (M.D. Fla. Mar. 19, 2012).

[72] Complaint, *FTC v. Broadway Global Master, Inc.*, No. 2:12-cv-855 (E.D. Cal. Apr. 3, 2012); *see also* Press Release, Court Halts Fake Debt Collector Calls from India, Grants FTC Request to Stop Defendants Who Posed as Law Enforcers (Apr. 11, 2012), *available at* http://www.ftc.gov/opa/2012/04/broadway.shtm.

[73] U.S. Dep't of Justice, Press Release, Tracy Man Indicted for Phony Debt Collection Scam (Aug. 23, 2012), *available at* http://www.justice.gov/usao/cae/news/docs/2012/08-2012/08-23-12Patel.html.

[74] *See* http://www.ftc.gov/opa/2012/08/amicus.shtm.

[75] *See FTC, Repairing a Broken System: Protecting Consumers in Debt Collection Litigation and Arbitration at 25-28 (July 2010), available at* http://www.ftc.gov/os/2010/07/debtcollectionreport.pdf.

[76] *United States v. Asset Acceptance, LLC*, No. 8:12-cv-182-T-27EAJ (M.D. Fla. Jan. 31, 2012) (court entered order); *see also* Press Release, Under FTC Settlement, Debt Buyer Agrees to Pay $2.5 Million for Alleged Consumer Deception (Jan. 30, 2012), *available at* http://www.ftc.gov/opa/2012/01/asset.shtm.

[77] *See* http://www.ftc.gov/os/closings/staff/120827rjmclosingletter.pdf.

[78] *Welcome to the FTC's Home for Consumer Information* (Dec. 2012), *available at* www.consumer.ftc.gov/blog/welcome-ftcs-home-consumer-information.

[79] FTC, *Fake Debt Collectors* (Feb. 2012), *available at* www.consumer.ftc.gov/articles/0258-fake-debt-collectors.

[80] *FTC, Time-Barred Debts* (Jan. 2012), *available at* www.consumer.ftc.gov/articles/0117-time-barred-debts.

[81] Federal Trade Commission Annual Report 2010: Fair Debt Collection Practices Act at 17, available at http://www.ftc.gov/os/2010/04/P104802fdcpa2010annrpt.pdf; FTC, Collecting Consumer Debts: The Challenges of Change at iv-v; 21-24 (Feb. 2009), available at http://www.ftc.gov/bcp/workshops/debtcollection/dcwr.pdf.

[82] The final transcript of the workshop is available at www.ftc.gov/bcp/workshops/debtcollectiontech/docs/transcript.pdf.

[83] These numbers are current through September 2012. The online access numbers reflect access of materials from the FTC's website and other official sources. They do not include access to materials that are downloaded from FTC channels and reposted on outside websites.

[84] The Term "All FTC Complaints" refers to all industry-specific complaints received by the FTC in a given calendar year. It excludes identify theft and Do Not Call Registry complaints.

INDEX

U

V

W

Y